FALL HARD, BOUNCE BACK STRONGER

A story of hardship, despair, and fight back

Book One

Marner Housen

FALL HARD, BOUNCE BACK STRONGER

A story of hardship, despair, and fight back

Marner Housen

Published by:

Joy of Many Generations Ltd.
info@joyofmanygenerations.com
Telephone: +44 (0) 7914 945 246
www.joyofmanygenerations.com

ISBN: 978-1-916667-15-0

TABLE OF CONTENTS

FOREWORD

This book is an amazing read. It reminds us of the wonderful love of God in all our situations. It also reminds us of our humanity, with our feelings and understanding. Yet, it also makes us humble and encourages us to always hang on to God's word in our lives. That no matter how big our mountains may seem to appear, God is with us and loves us through it all.

Thankfully, the author has included continuous scripture references throughout the book, which should resonate well with readers at different points in their lives. These verses serve as a daily reminder that our God is great, and He cares about us. And through Him, all things are possible.

I am truly grateful for the opportunity to read and write the foreword for this awesome book. It has not only rekindled my love for reading meaningful Christian literature but I also hope it will inspire and strengthen your faith in the same way. May God bless you abundantly as you read and reflect upon these words.

Ana Odendaal
Manager and
Nursery educator.

INTRODUCTION

Do you ever wish you could rewrite the past or some chapters of your life? I certainly do. However, no one really gets the opportunity to; but you do get the opportunity to make better choices that could impact future outcomes positively.

Over the years, I have met and worked with countless numbers of people across a wide spectrum in society who have been given—or unfortunately chosen—a bad set of cards, yet they still managed to play the cards and win. Alternately, there were others with the same set of cards who played but didn't win initially. If you are one of them, don't give up, take courage. Some of life's greatest lessons and successes are experienced by those who didn't hit the bull's eye in the first round.

Life is unpredictable and full of mysteries. Like Allison, whose story you'll soon discover, at times you might have to seek refuge in a cave whilst the world is closing in on you. But you should never underestimate the power of seemingly insignificant things —like a spider that can spin a beautiful web across your cave helping to cover your tracks.

Hence, if you have to take refuge in a cave, or can't even explain how you got in there, take courage; you will emerge a victor. If life tastes like marmite or sour strawberries and you don't like the taste, keep spitting it out until you discover the flavour that truly satisfies you. And if you fall or stumble while running in a race, don't waste time crying! Get back up —It's time to bounce back stronger.

That's what this book is about - the crises people face in life and how they overcame them because they learnt to let go and let the Divine take over. Never underestimate the invisible Divine force at work in the universe that sees, feels and wants to ease your pain, if only you will permit it. That's why this book draws on examples from the Divine Book of Treasures to encourage you to seek and tap into the kind of help that can never fail.

Help from that source will stop every form of unwanted situations in your life, bringing victory, love, joy, peace, hope and life's fulfilment.

As you open up to the contents of this book, you will be equipped with the tools that will empower you not to despair, but to bounce back from every fall or circumstance that you might have experienced.

> *Whether you have been given, or you have unfortunately chosen a bad set of cards, you can play and still win.*

1

UNEXPLAINED CIRCUMSTANCES

One morning whilst travelling to work on a packed tube on the London underground network, I looked up and saw an advertisement with the picture of a wounded dog. It read: *Urgent appeal, Animal welfare crisis:*

> *Shot six times.*
> *Beaten with a shovel.*
> *Dumped in a ditch.*

It continued, *"Rocky was shot with an air rifle and left for dead – yet this brave dog fought to survive. Eventually, he was rescued and got the expert care that saved his life. Will you help care for animals like Rocky – when no one else will?"*

Saddened, I began to feel a surge of different emotions – anger, empathy, hopelessness and disappointment – racing like horses on a track through every fibre of my being as I tried to imagine the screams, the cries, the howling and helplessness of poor Rocky as it experienced this terrible ordeal. I could almost sense the viciousness coupled with the unfeeling and uncaring manner of its owner as the sound of the last bullet echoed in the thin air. It then dawned on me that we humans experience this same kind of ordeal too, and the sadness of it all gripped me with fright all over again.

At times, life can be filled with troubles and heartaches. Sometimes we create and bring them upon ourselves, other times, they just seem to happen suddenly and indiscriminately. When this occurs, we refer to them as unpredictable major life events. However, regardless of how they came about and what impact they might have created; we are often encouraged not to cry but to get up. You can bounce back from every situation no matter how hard you might have fallen, or how hopeless, disabling and distressing it may seem.

But, how can one do this, you might ask? Is it possible? Of course! You were designed by the Creator of the universe with resilience, greatness and insight on the inside. In times of trouble and turbulence, the light within often gets covered by the darkness you are encountering. But don't panic! Everyone at some point experiences dark situations including the Creator of the universe but you must refuse to stay there. Get up and declare what you want to experience, then the universe will align with your positive declarations and compel the darkness to flee. As this begins to happen, the path ahead of you will be illuminated, enabling you to exit the maze of life.

Still on the long tube commute, I looked around at the people sitting, reading their newspapers, whilst others stood, listening to music and chatting, oblivious to the sound in my head and the advertisement posted in front of their eyes. Then, in the midst of my thoughts, I suddenly saw something flashed in front of me. I couldn't believe it. It was a machine with some instructions written all around it, on top were three coloured buttons with flashing lights. I quickly leaned over to read:

"By pressing one of these three buttons on this time machine, you can be transported into the past, the future or—who knows—maybe someplace entirely unexpected? Press one of them and describe the world in which you find yourself."

I was amazed at what I had just read. At first, it felt real, like I was sitting in a large packed examination room with other students, anxiously waiting to write an English examination essay, and having no clue what to write.

Then I turned again and looked, and there it was, the words were staring at me almost like the piercing eyes of an owl in the dark. My heart began to pound. I could also feel a pulsing in my wrists and a compelling urge to press one of the buttons. Then, the machine seemed to be disappearing before my eyes like a mist. In a frantic move, I quickly stretched out my arm and barely managed to grab one of the buttons and pressed it.

Suddenly, I found myself in the countryside, looking up at the stars in the night skies and breathing in the fresh sea breeze. I reached over and shut the window, pulled the cover over my head, and lay there trying to figure out which button I had pressed.

You can bounce back from every situation no matter how hard you might have fallen, or how hopeless, disabling and distressing it may seem.

2

A DOUBLE SURPRISE

With the sun's rays streaming through the window pane, I suddenly woke to the sweet sound of singing parakeets amidst other birds and bees competing for space on the laden fruit trees out in the orchard. The smell of fresh ripe fruits was everywhere. There were mangoes, tangerines, pineapples, berries, guavas, bananas among others. I quickly closed my eyes then opened them again and asked myself, is this real?

Then in a couple of minutes, the bustling sound outside was quickly drowned out by the sweet melodies of a live guitar playing to a tune and a melody of the buzzing nature that filled the morning. It felt like I was wide awake in a dream, but no, it was real. With one eye peeping through the covers, I looked up and I was stunned. I thought I was hallucinating. I didn't know what to think. I was surrounded and serenaded by five guitarists led by my childhood sweetheart, Les. I was petrified. I was speechless. I had not seen Les in years since we both immigrated. It was like a dream come true seeing him again. We couldn't stop embracing each other and with that, the staff quickly hurried out of the way. I didn't even have time to change out of my nightgown, and it never seemed to matter.

A few hours later, I came to realise that Les has been a widower for five years. He had been left on his own to raise his fraternal twin children, Vin and Vanessa, who were of primary school age. They too were wide awake and it seemed like they were just waiting for their daddy's signal. Suddenly, they came racing towards me with excitement and came straight into my arms, yelling "Mom!" "Mom!" "Mom!" as if I were their real biological mother. Their attitude was so perfect, as if they were acting out a rehearsed script, and maybe they were. It could also be the natural, sincere yearn that little children have for the love of a mother in their lives. Whatever the reason, their little warm embrace felt so real, so normal and sincere that I was moved with compassion and love. I was touched by their warmth; their excitement, their cuddles and the fact that they had no one to call 'mother' except me.

It was amazing. I was showered with hugs and kisses all over. It felt like an act of sheer honesty and innocence, the kind that one gets when interacting with little children. They adjusted so quickly to me as if I was their biological mother who had come back to life. I guess it was their natural instinct, that natural desire that comes from being genetically wired for attachment. I quickly thought to myself, they really need a new mother. They needed someone to nurture and love them, and I was ready to assume that role. My mind was even racing ahead of time and I began to feel fortunate to have met them.

Nine months later, Vinn and Vanessa played the roles of page boy and flower girl at our wedding. Les and I were so pleased and fortunate to watch them enjoying their roles. It still feels so surreal. I told myself, if this was a dream, I didn't want to wake up.

About a month later, Les took them into the city to spend the night with their grandmother, Mama Tamer, who was leaving in a few days for a month-long charity trip out of the country.

I planned to pick them up from school the following day whilst Les was at work.

Being alone that morning, I looked out from our plateau and spotted Uncle Sam's café. I could also distinguish the smell of ripe fruits amidst the scent of freshly brewed, spiced coffee and hot cinnamon buns even a mile away. Or was it just my imagination? With the hot caramel-glazed cinnamon buns on my mind, I raced out of bed without a second to spare, washed, quickly got dressed and queued, waiting to be served.

Everyone was talking, seemingly concerned about what had happened the day before in this farming village. I quickly grabbed the local newspaper, and there it was, in the headlines:

Village farmer battling for life after trying to rescue wayward sheep.

Then it continued:

They say sheep know their Shepherd's voice, but this one seemed a stranger indeed! Ruddy was always different. He had a mind of his own; always playful but wayward. Papa John, at eighty, the oldest Shepherd in the village, suddenly realised that his favourite sheep was missing from the flock. It was late evening and he wanted to herd them into the barn. As he looked over to where his neighbours' sheep were, there stood Ruddy looking over at him. Like a happy child, he came running towards Papa John but fell into a pond. In a frantic effort to save him, Papa John rushed forward and jumped in after him immediately. But soon, he found himself struggling but he held on to Ruddy and screamed for help. Now, poor Papa John is in intensive care in hospital battling for his life.

Everyone in the village loved Papa John, and now they are all terrified. Will he recover?

As I sat there waiting to be served the hot cinnamon bun, I was thinking how horrible it would be if Papa John lost his life and the impact it would have on his family and the villagers as a whole. I could also remember a Sunday school lesson from some years ago, told by an old vicar with a long white beard, leaning on his walking stick. As he read from the book of Isaiah and began to speak, fear crept into our little hearts as we listened to his warnings about the dangers of waywardness. Reverend Frestos used the analogy of sheep and the good Shepherd as an illustration, and I began to make connections.

In summation, he told us that as innocent as we were, we need to be careful as we mature, not to become side-tracked, because young individuals are usually vulnerable to group influence. Consequently, when that happens, we tend to follow the group rather than heed the wisdom of the Good Shepherd in staying on the right path of life. We would rather hang out with our friends than spending time in The Shepherd's care so that he could lead us. Therefore, the Good Shepherd, in reminding us of our vulnerability, had said, *"Like sheep we often strayed; we have left the path to follow our own way." (Isaiah 53:6 KJV paraphrased.)* When we do this, like Ruddy, we expose ourselves to the dangers of the waters of life, and endanger the lives of others too.

Whilst I was still reading the newspaper and thinking about it, my mind drifted to Allison, a law student who went to a very prestigious private school but attended the same university as us. I had not seen her since we graduated from university but she had left an indelible print on my mind. It was strange though, like lightning she had just flashed through my mind. However, I had no doubt that she would be fine wherever she was.

Allison, an only child, was from an upper middle-class family and she always has a calm air of graciousness about her. Both of her parents were professionals. Her father was the CEO of a large chartered accounting firm and her mother was a gifted surgeon and professor. They were also affiliated with politics. Adding to that, they co-owned an automobile company and a small fleet of budget airlines. Consequently, Allison flew out of the country every half term along with most weekends. In her dormitory room, she had a world map and at age 19, she had marked off dozens of cities she had visited around the world in between her studies. How she did it, I don't know, but she was an avid reader.

She was also very organised, focused and responsible, qualities I presumed she inherited from her role model parents. Allison hated the idea of procrastinating and I presumed she got it from them too. Hence, her parents never restricted her travels because she maintained consistently high grades throughout her studies. Additionally, she volunteered for humanitarian projects, including helping to serve hot meals to the homeless at a local walk-in cafeteria and donating textbooks and items of clothing to the less fortunate. We often used to ask her how she found time to do everything, and she would always laugh and say it was easy. She always told us that you have to develop a routine that works for you.

We used to crowd Allison's dormitory room prior to an upcoming party, ball or any other event on or off campus, because her dresses were exquisite. They were purchased during stopovers in major cities around the world. If you were looking for it, she had it – whatever it was from London, Paris, Milan, New York, Sydney and elsewhere in the world. It was incredible. Her wardrobe overflowed with beaded pearl dresses, lace, fine Egyptian linens and just about anything from the latest fashion line. Indeed, she was a girl of sophistication and elegance, and the "bling-bling" as they now call it.

During a special occasion or event, one could spot Allison from a distance with her shoulders squared and walking with the perfect gait, as if she were on a catwalk in Paris. Yet, she did it all with quiet confidence, elegance and humility. She was also incredibly beautiful and well liked on campus. This was partly because she was very personable, compassionate, comical and kind, especially to those who were less fortunate than her. Allison was a very wonderful person indeed!

I have very fond memories of her including one of her ballroom dresses that I borrowed and never returned. It is still hanging in my wardrobe.

> *Like sheep, we often stray; we have left the path to follow our own way." (Isaiah 53:6 KJV paraphrased.)*

3

A FALL FROM GRACE

"Beg you a dollar, sir", I heard as I sat tucking into my hot cinnamon bun dripping with sticky toffee caramel. The tone seemed camouflaged but I could still hear the perfect diction beneath the desperation of hunger in the somewhat nervous voice. As the voice came closer and closer, begging along the rows of tables, I looked up and couldn't believe my eyes. I thought I was hallucinating. I thought my sight needed corrective lenses. I didn't know what to think. "Oh no!" I thought to myself. "It's Allison." "Allison?" "Could it be Allison?" Out of fright and uncertainty, I began to quickly conceal the shock on my face as she stood over me and said, "Beg you a dollar ma'am." I looked up at her and she stared down at me. "You look familiar to me," I said quietly. "I believe I have seen you somewhere." She looked at me with her piercing hazel eyes and was about to move on when I reached for my handbag.

I tried to wipe the sticky caramel from my fingers before attempting to open my purse. She waited in anticipation with her eyes fixed on me. During the process, I quietly asked her, "Are you Allie?" "Allie, is that you?" That's what we used to call her at university. She smiled faintly and I could see the embarrassment creeping onto her face as she began to recognise me. I was so shocked yet so happy to see her. In an attempt to reconnect as we used to, I quickly transitioned to a friendlier upbeat tone. "Girl, what are you doing here? So, this is where you hang out, eh?" She looked at me more puzzled, mortified and confused. However, she kept staring at me as if she was listening to a drama queen. She seemed uninterested and appeared to be lost in her own little world. I immediately realised how insensitive I was.

Allison was desperate for a dollar, eager to get it and move on, whilst I was desperate to reconnect with her. Her body language seemed to be urging me on, but my hand suddenly froze in my purse because I couldn't believe what I was seeing. I thought to myself, how bizarre! She had just flashed through my mind earlier and now, here she was.

I signalled to Ted, the waiter, then pulled out my purse slowly. She stood still and waited as I opened my purse exposing paper notes and coins. I took a few notes into my hands and started counting them, then stopped to pull out a chair beside me. Her full hazel eyes dazzled in amazement at the notes and she was totally oblivious of what I was doing. I was trying to offer her a seat in the meantime. Just then, Ted interrupted, "Is that all you wanted Madam?" I nodded in confirmation and gave the notes to him as he served the table with another hot cinnamon bun dripping with glazed sticky toffee caramel and a cup of hot chocolate, complemented with some fresh strawberries. I could sense a mixture of disappointment and respite as Allison slumped into the chair, with her eyes still following the notes in Ted's hands. Then came a sigh of relief as if she had just completed a long-distance walking competition and was desperately in need of rest and hydration.

I knew it would compel her to stay as it was one of our favourite snacks, we girls used to have during study breaks at Kirk's café across the road from our dormitory at university.

Allison looked down at the tray with the cinnamon bun, then up at me, as if unsure whose it was. I moved the tray closer to her. As she took it, I heard someone shouting to Ted, "Ted! This woman comes here too often begging, you need to keep her out! This is not the kind of place for beggars. You will lose your customers!" On and on, he ranted. We ignored the rant as I was too happy to see Allison, and too curious to catch up with her.

In the meantime, I wanted to politely remind Allison that there was a restroom in the corner near our table where she could wash her hands, but she was too quick. With caramel already dripping all over her fingers and her tongue mopping it all up, I realised the reminder would have been too late. Allison ate as if she hadn't eaten in two months. Forgive me, but my auntie Essie would say, she ate like a pig.

Suddenly, I felt an unusual silence in the café. I glanced up and all eyes were on our table. They looked at me as if I had done something wrong but I ignored the piercing eyes, not knowing that Allison had previously harassed diners and stolen from the café. She had even tried to intimidate one of the workers for food whilst he was in the process of serving other diners.

Then came the slurp and you could hear the rumbling sound of the hot chocolate settling down her empty stomach like a rapid stream hitting pebbles beneath, Or better still, like sudden autumn rains on a zinc roof. Then it was all over. I couldn't believe it! Two minutes, and breakfast was finished. Like a parched flower that has been revived from the sudden downpour of rain, so was Allison's Sahara-like dessert appearance. The breakfast revived her. Now she looked at me with puzzled eyes and great unease as if saying, "What am I doing sitting here?" "I am not allowed. Do you not know? Just give me the dollar and ease me out of my pain and misery."

Allie, "Are you ok?" I asked. I then thought, with the rapid speed at which she ate, she must be craving for more. I enquired, "Would you like a full breakfast?" She nodded in the affirmative and I placed the order immediately.

I knew something was wrong. This was not the "prim and proper" Allison I knew. The high flier, affluent Allison. The Allison who handed out cash to us like her parents were picking it off the streets. The Allison whose wardrobe was so packed that she lost count of her possessions. The Allison who flew out of the country as often as one boarding a bus to work every day. The Allison who taught social graces to many from disadvantaged backgrounds in our clubs and debating societies on campus. Now, she seemed to need a refresher course herself. Adding to that, she had scratches and bruises all over. Like Rocky, she looked beaten, battered, dumped and left for dead. Combined with the type of fabric print that she was wearing, her attire looked synonymous with someone who had fallen into a ditch. No wonder all eyes were on us in the café as she sat at my table.

It became obvious that the glamour and pearl laces had disappeared. She now walked with a slight limp and smelt of tobacco mixed with other strong substances. To give her the benefit of the doubt, she seemed to have sat by the roadside with others smoking around her, or maybe she had just started to experiment. Her smile was no longer perfect as one of her canines was missing. I then began to ask myself, what could have happened? What could have gone so wrong? Like Ruddy, the playful but wayward sheep that had fallen into the pond and endangered both itself and its owner, Papa John, could it be that Allison had become wayward and fallen in the ponds of life and, like the sheep, was unable to swim out? Could it be that her waywardness had caused her parents much grief and loss, and now she is left vulnerable?

Why was this once glamourous girl, now looking so unkempt? Where are her parents? Are they still alive? Is she in touch with them? Do they still have the family businesses? So many questions raced through my mind as I sat and watched her tucking into a proper breakfast of toast topped with cream cheese, smoked salmon and grilled tomatoes. This was accompanied by freshly brewed hazelnut-flavoured coffee, a medium-sized bowl of oats porridge with a mixture of fresh berries and a glass of orange juice. As she ate, her countenance lit up as if she was eating from a buffet table. I was intrinsically moved.

Allison used to be so wealthy. She had it all. Now it seems like she has lost it all. Where did it all go wrong? I presumed she didn't have a plan after graduating. She had a better yesterday.

Curiosity was now getting the better of me as I sat waiting for her to finish her breakfast. I couldn't wait to engage her in a conversation. I wanted to know. I wanted to hear. I wanted to understand. I wanted to listen to her story and I wanted her to give me the opportunity to do so.

> *Things do change. Today, a situation of "Beg you a dollar, sir" can later become "How best can I invest these hard earned dollars?"*

4

A TERRIBLE INCIDENT

It was nearing lunchtime and I still hadn't given Allison the dollar she begged for earlier. Surprisingly, she wasn't looking as desperate as before. Perhaps it was because she had eaten a balanced meal. However, at regular intervals, she kept eyeing my purse. Often, she would look up at the beautiful wall paintings in front of us in the café, other times, at the queue as people placed their orders, then back at my purse. She seemed to be on watch constantly. Then suddenly, it was as if her eyes turned into an x-ray machine and I couldn't figure out whether she wanted to grab my purse and run or whether she was worried about the next customer who she might not want to see. I couldn't understand why she seemed 'on edge'. The unease was too obvious. But then I thought, why not, when she has been "in trouble'' with a few people in the café and around the area lately.

We left the café. She followed me like a lamb going to the slaughter. Nobody had given her anything or even tried to entertain her, it seemed, so I knew it was her desperation that kept her by my side. Nevertheless, I thought I shouldn't give her the money just yet. If I did, she would probably disappear immediately and I wouldn't see her again or get to hear her story. So, I clutched my multi-coloured, red, green and orange leather handbag tightly underneath my arm. We walked for five minutes to the park down the road overlooking the beach.

As we walked, I could hear the following words of scripture vibrating in my head like a bass drum:

> *"Do not withhold good from those to whom it is due,*
> *When it is in the power of your hand to do so.*
> *Do not say to your neighbour,*
> *"Go, and come back,*
> *And tomorrow I will give it,"*
> *When you have it with you." (Proverbs 3:27-28 NKJV).*

I was amazed. At first, it was like a gentle nudge, but the more I ignored it, the louder and louder it came crashing into my head as if it wanted to drive me insane with guilt. I was petrified, but I kept calm and tried to drown it out with more conversations as we kept walking.

Have you ever been in a situation where you knew the right thing to do yet you didn't do it? Sometimes it might be out of fear, reluctance or rationalization. Whatever the reason, it is not good. As the scripture reminds us,

> *"Therefore, to him that knoweth to do good, and doeth it not, to him it is   sin." (James 4:17 KJV)*

As we walked on, we decided to cross the road at the traffic lights. Feeling rather impatient to wait until the lights change, we dashed across the road trying to beat an oncoming white van. Then, as I mounted the sidewalk, I could hear the screeching sound of sharp brakes followed by a loud "bang!" I was frightened and had concluded in my mind that someone was probably hit and had died. Then I turned quickly to check whether Allison was beside me, but she wasn't.

I screamed. "Allie! Allie! Allison! Where are you?" I turned around and I was alarmed. I screamed in fright again. There she was, sprawled in the middle of the road on her back with legs apart - helpless. "I knew it! I knew it!" I said in my mind. "She didn't see the ripe banana peel as she ran across the road." No one prepared us for what would follow next. The driver exited the white van in rage. For a moment, I wondered whether he was intoxicated, but then I thought, it might be out of fright. His van was smashed and the traffic lights knocked down. Allison had bruises to her arms and legs, and I was sure she was hit.

Immediately, memories of my aunt's children—Clover and Clemsie—flooded back. They had been hit on their way to school, and one of them hadn't survived.

Oblivious to what was happening, I wondered why the driver was so hostile to Allison. I tried to call 999, but he threatened, "I'll beat you! Drop that phone or else!" He then reached over to fetch something from inside his white van and I threw the phone immediately into my handbag. I was shaking. I thought, "You won't hurt us and you won't win either." I hoped one of the passers-by would intervene and call the police on our behalf. Meanwhile, I couldn't stop wondering who this man was. Maybe he was reacting out of shock. Maybe he had been dozing behind the wheel. Maybe he had been distracted by his phone. Maybe he crashed because he was trying to avoid hitting Allison. Whatever the reason, he was far too irate and uncouth for me to make sense of his behaviour. Still frightened and shaking, I kept thinking that there was no need for such a strong level of aggression towards a pedestrian. His level of anger was such that I thought his heart would soon explode.

Then as I listened, I began to understand. "I could have run you over," he said. "You always think I wanted to kill you but I had my opportunity today. It's another great day for you, eh!" "You are lucky not to be alone." I couldn't believe what I was hearing.

"Don't touch me!" exclaimed Allison as he tried to help her up. I quickly dragged her out of the road and onto the sidewalk. Luckily, there was no oncoming traffic. We then sat at the empty bus stop directly opposite where Allison had fallen. From our encounter at the café, it was clear that Allison's physical appearance already bore massive signs of suffering. This man didn't need to add to it, I thought. However, Allison didn't shed a tear. It seemed like she had become hardened to suffering. This was a complete contradiction to the once sophisticated, gentle and understanding person who was full of finesse and was "living the life."

The man got back into his van and all we could hear was the revving of the engine. It wouldn't start and he began swearing and shouting at Allison saying, "See what this stupid woman has caused! She always causes bad things to happen to me." Then he picked up his phone presumably to call either his insurance company or someone he knew for assistance to tow his vehicle. He wasn't even showing any signs of gratitude that he was not hurt. I was even surprised too, because, up to that point, no emergency vehicle had arrived.

A few people passed by and saw what had happened but it appeared like no one had a phone. They also showed no concern or empathy. No one asked any questions. Maybe, they too were frightened by his annoyance and threats or they were caught up into their own little world. In despair, I said to Allison, "Good Samaritans seem to be on the decline these days."

However, through all this, I was only concerned about Allison's welfare. She kept reassuring me that she wasn't hit and that she was only feeling a burning sensation from the bruises on the palm of her hands and legs. I thought she might still be in shock. Then amidst the cursing and swearing about his insurance; under clenched teeth, Allison said to me quietly, "It's my estranged husband. It's Frankie."

Allison paused for a moment, then continued, her voice steady but filled with emotion: "Elsie, it seemed like there is always some 'special event' that keeps bringing me and this man together. It's like a country's major events like the Olympics, trade fairs or the world cup that happens repeatedly. The only difference is that, those events are positive and bring benefits. Frankie's attitude to me can be likened to a dangerous virus. You can't see it coming, but can only experience its impact which is always detrimental. It continues to separate us. We have been separated for years now and ever since, a sequence of unusual events like this one kept bringing us back together. As a matter of fact, since we got together, our lives never fail to experience some form of incident or drama."

"I don't know if you had realised then, that's why I was always 'on edge' in the café wondering if he would stop to grab a sandwich then pounce on me." Allison continued. "He is the virus I feared. I haven't seen him in a long while but it seemed like only yesterday. It seemed like he wanted to finish off what he started. He even tried to kill me when we were abroad on holiday and on a few other occasions when we were living together."

As Allison spoke, my attentive listening seemed to encourage her, and she began to open up to me like a morning glory flower.

We then ditched our plans to continue to the park as Allison's legs had become stiff and swollen with dried blood crusting over the bruises she sustained. Instead, we stayed at the bus stop trying to make sense of what had just happened. The enclosed bus stop shielded us from further public embarrassment.

As Allison continued speaking, one could hear the subtle anger in her voice even amidst the sudden surge of autumn breeze caressing our dresses and turning them into swirling balloons. Goosebumps covered all over our skins as we shivered in the chill. Meanwhile, Frankie was absorbed in a phone conversation in which he was angrily shouting at someone about what had happened to his white van. I quickly called a cab, eager to get away in search of warmth and safety.

We ended up in a comfy, elegant café nestled in the lobby area of a travel hotel. I ordered a latte, an Americano white with a blueberry muffin and a white chocolate cherry muffin. We then sat in the furthest corner near a window. The waiter eyed Allison as if she didn't belong but we ignored her and settled in. I thought to myself, it's the colour and unusual print of her dress. Go away' I thought to myself. "Nothing is wrong with her. She is not as dirty as you think."

Before being served, Allison located the restroom and she cleaned the bruises. I followed behind her and assisted with band aid and alcohol swabs. She had minor swellings and bruises that just needed some first aid treatment. As a mom with two very active twins, I was always prepared with first aid for any minor events. As the bruises dried, Allison mentioned her legs feeling a bit stiffer but she didn't dwell on it.

Allison carried on talking. Then she looked directly into my eyes and asked, "Elsie, what should you do when there are surprise questions on the exam papers of life?" I felt very cheeky and wanted to say, "It only happens when you haven't been well prepared." However, I understood her context clearly and I responded, "It's not unusual, and many times, there are no immediate answers." Then the tears began to flow and I came to realise that this gracious law student I once knew on campus was in fact deeply hurting.

Then she interrupted my thoughts with another question. "What would you do if you were ahead in a 100m sprint athletics race and suddenly, someone deliberately elbowed you from behind causing you to lose momentum and fall?" She continued, "Then the athlete who elbowed you carried on running and still received the gold medal. No disqualification, no penalties or rebuke given, as if nobody saw what happened on camera?"

Upon saying this, Allison's piercing hazel eyes seemed to change colour and she began to look and sound like a lioness being robbed of her cubs. "Life isn't fair!" "Life isn't fair!" She yelled as tears welled up in her eyes. I reassured her that I understood how she felt, but, maybe, life wasn't meant to be fair either. Then I launched into a discourse with her.

"You know, Allison," I began, "In this day and age that we are now living in, one doesn't even have to pre-empt fights. They just present themselves in one form or another. It's called the storms of life. They are turbulent and they come without warning."

Our dear bishop would often say, *"Life is not a fun-fare, it is warfare."* Therefore, I believe that in life, one has to learn the tactics of war and how to fight to win and keep winning. This means, one has to settle it within oneself that life is a warfare and that people will use any strategy to win a war, including unfair means. That is why countries are monitored with regards to their use of chemical weapons because using chemical weapons to fight is not fighting fairly.

I have witnessed fair physical fights when I was in primary and secondary school and personally, I didn't like to see them occur as I was too scared. I also never engage in any because I don't think it's an art that I could master due to fear and lack of interest. Personally, I tend to view fights as an abuse and violation of another person's individuality and dignity, whether it is of a malicious nature or done for professional entertainment. In primary or secondary school, two students would start to throw fists at each other, and everyone would watch to see who would win. Nobody would intervene unless one was at risk.

Now-a-days, people gang fight one individual or use weapons to assist them and no one intervenes to save the victim. Fairness, empathy, forgiveness, love and compassion seem to have taken wings, and have flown out of the hearts of many individuals like migratory birds. Life seems to be like that these days. Hence, life is not fair, it's a constant battle for many people.

Elsie's words flowed with passion, and it was clear that Allison, though still recovering from her emotional storm, was listening intently. 'You see, Allison,' Elsie continued, in battles, you have to study your opponents and learn battle strategies to win. Sometimes you might not win all the battles that come against you in life and often, you need to ignore many of them, because some are traps. Traps designed to make you fall into the pits of life. For instance, there are traps of distraction; traps of wasting valuable time and traps of diversion of destinies, among others. However, in spite of it all, you can still win the war and that should be your main focus. One translation puts it this way about Jesus, *"Because he never lost sight of where he was headed—that exhilarating finish in and with God—he could put up with anything along the way: Cross, shame, whatever. And now he's there, in the place of honour, right alongside God. (Hebrews 12:2 MSG)*

Although fights should be avoided as much as possible, yet there are times we need to fight, but we should do so wisely. From observing fights, and being involved in a few verbal ones, I have noticed that some people are like skunks, after the fight is over, they leave you stinking. People will leave you stinking in terms of character assassination, lies and mischief especially when they don't emerge as victors. Therefore, you have to choose your battles carefully. As the Book of Instruction states, *"Strategic planning is the key to warfare; to win, you need a lot of good counsel. (Proverbs 24:6 MSG)*. Elsie paused for a moment, making sure that the weight of what she had said was sinking in. She added, therefore, never forget or underestimate God's divine, invisible forces that are at work on your side at all times.

Elsie continued; her voice thoughtful as she reflected on the lessons of life. "I once watched a short video clip of some tourists at a zoo. A young child seemed uninterested to go on the tour with his parents, so he was left sitting, playing with a toy and enjoying himself with his back leaning on the glass fence of one section of the zoo. It was in that section that the tigers were caged. I'm sure the zoo keeper kept them well fed. However, due to their natural instincts, one of the tigers came to the glass fence. Upon seeing the child, it began biting and clawing at the glass with his paws. Then, in a fit of rage, it opened its mouth ferociously, and lunged at the glass, as if trying to get to the toddler. It had so much anger and energy as if it hadn't been fed for months.

All this time, it was desperately trying to devour the child who was oblivious to what was happening behind him. The more engrossed the child got in playing with his toy, the angrier the tiger became. The child never saw the tiger, therefore didn't have any reason to be scared or alarmed by it. I am sure that if he saw what was happening behind him, he would have thrown away his toy, screamed and dashed to his parents for safety.

"Like that child," Elsie explained, "this is what God does for us with His goodness and mercy that is always following and protecting us from the invisible enemies that are waging wars against us without our knowledge. They are relentless in their attempt to claw at us, viciously trying to devour us. Yet, God's invisible hands shield us. Not only will He help us to overcome life's battles, he will also repay us for the unfair treatment that we have suffered. As it is written, *"All this trouble is a clear sign that God has decided to make you fit for the kingdom. You're suffering now, but justice is on the way. In his justice he will pay back those who persecute you."* *(2 Thessalonians 1: 5 MSG; 2 Thessalonians 6 NLT).*

 What that glass fence was to that child, the Lord himself is to us each and every day. *"The LORD himself will fight for you. Just stay calm." (Exodus 14:14 NLT)*

Elsie continued, "Allison, take courage. It won't be long before you are vindicated and restored. Isn't it interesting? When we are right, we demand justice. When we are wrong, we plead from mercy. In life, at times we find ourselves on either side of the fence, so don't give up. Don't let the tears hold you back either. That's life. Just get up and keep going.

> *Always remember, even the most terrible incident can be turned into a terrific one. It's a matter of perspective.*

5

CAREER REFLECTION

Allison took a slow breath, the emotion in her voice unmistakable as she began to share her story.

"My father suddenly developed a rare disease that affected both his mobility and mental state, so mum hired two nurses to assist him. His care was very expensive but mum never mind paying as they could afford it. The disease usually strikes people in the prime of their lives, between the ages of thirty and fifty and dad was diagnosed with it at age fifty. It's called Huntington's disease. Mum carried on working at first but later stopped to help with dad's personal care. She felt that as both his wife, and a surgeon, she should be the one caring for dad instead of caring for other patients in the hospital.

As dad was the primary financier of the family, mum had entrusted everything in his care. Now that he was mentally incapacitated, mum could no longer access the key to his brain via communication so as to unlock the treasure of our family's fortune. In the meantime, I worked at a huge law firm for several years but I wasn't enjoying it. It became too demanding.

At times, people are not aware that in law, there are many deadlines to meet, clients' demands, long hours, changing laws, evolving legal technologies etc. and one has to put aside one's personal interest to keep abreast of these changes. By then, my dad had become one of my personal interests and I wasn't getting the opportunity to see him regularly or to travel as often as I used to. So, I decided to change careers, and teaching seemed like a feasible option. I thought it would better meet my personal needs based on the much-coveted holidays, so I switched to teaching.

As Elsie listened to Allison, she was thinking, "girl, get real!" "Welcome to the real world where personal interests often get side-lined too. It's a world where your holidays get planned for you with set breaks and all. It's a world filled with a ton of preparation, marking, pastoral responsibilities and endless admin duties."

"Teaching?" I exclaimed sarcastically. "Yes!" Allison replied. "When I thought of the holidays, I couldn't resist."

Allison continued, "As soon as I applied, I got the job immediately at a college to teach criminology. I didn't have any formal teaching qualification per se. However, in hindsight, maybe that's what I should have studied with you girls at university, but of course, my law degree sufficed for the post.

Within the first few weeks on the job, I was already way ahead with my holiday planning. I booked a Caribbean cruise and I didn't say a word to any of my colleagues in the department about it, after all, I was the newest team member. Then, to my dismay, within three weeks, I was flooded with scripts to take home for marking. It was then I later realised that teachers mark even during the Christmas holidays. How bizarre! "How am I going to cope with this?" I thought. "Am I going to take the scripts with me on the cruise too?"

Diplomatically, I asked Martin, one of the teachers, whether he marks scripts during the holidays.

Mrs. Fanny, a tall, elegantly dressed teacher with brownish grey hair, was eavesdropping. With her thin-wire framed glasses tilted at the tip of her nose, and with raised eyebrows, she interrupted in a rather sarcastic tone. "I'm afraid summer is the only true holiday you will ever get in teaching, dear." She continued, "These young, new generations of teachers, that's all they ever think about - the holidays." Then she chuckled and added, as if patronizing me, "Welcome to the noble profession, dear." None of us responded. She glanced up at us, and we looked down at her, as she continued marking some scripts at her desk.

I immediately felt a bit guilty at my reaction to her because I knew she was trying to "warm up" to me, but I wasn't mentally prepared for what she had to say. I wanted an escape route from my law career, and there she was, hinting that I had walked into a net, like a fish who had escaped from the hook and line but was now entangled in the net.

Allison took a pause, glancing at Elsie before continuing.

So, there I was, standing in the staffroom, and Joe, a student, stood at the staffroom door, and with excitement in his voice, yelled, "Miss! Miss! Have you marked our test papers yet? "Did I do well?"

Mrs Fanny, in a rather stern and abrupt tone snapped. "Joe! Boy! When did you take your test?" she demanded.

Joe, clearly stunned by her abrupt and feisty response, replied, "Yesterday, Miss."

Allison leaned back, gesturing animatedly as she continued. "So Mrs. Fanny looks up at Joe, and says, "Yes, you did your test yesterday and you are asking for the results today! "Have you forgotten the size of your class, Joe?" "It's 31. Yes! 31 and I have five different groups to mark."

Mrs Fanny's response hypnotized poor Joe.

Elsie let out a low whistle. "Ouch. Poor Joe."

Mrs Fanny continued, "What's wrong with these students?" "Do they think we teachers are machines?" She carried on ranting, "Do you not know that it is break time and we teachers deserve to have our break? "Do you also not know that you are not allowed at the staffroom door at this time? You will certainly serve detention for this later, Joe. "Do you hear me? See you in session 5."

And with that, she dismissed him instantly.

Allison continued, shaking her head as she remembered the scene, "I thought Mrs Fanny's response was a bit abrupt and harsh. I also wondered whether she was having a bad day, or whether she just wanted to impress me as a new member of the team. Whatever the reason, she should have known that the student was just asking out of sheer curiosity and eagerness to know his results.

"You know, Elsie," Allison continued in a moment of reflection, looking back on our own days as students, we didn't think of the processes involved in marking. We just wanted to know our scores. That's all. She paused, her tone softening. "In the meantime, I was praying that poor Joe wouldn't get discouraged and quit the course. Already, the course was predominantly female-dominated, he was the only male in a class of 31 students, so he needed all the inspiration he could get to keep going.

Joe, still with his eyes fixed on the staffroom floor in shock and embarrassment, suddenly looked up at her, then quietly turned and walked away.

Martin turned to me with a knowing look. "Allison, listen to her. Mrs. Fanny is firm, but she is a great teacher. She has more than thirty years of experience.

Sceptical, I asked, "Is that what makes a great teacher, Martin?

So, he said, "Wait! I am not finished yet. Mrs Fanny is always well prepared and she gives very prompt feedback to her students."

With a hint of sarcasm in my voice, I replied, "I hope that's not an example of her prompt feedback that we just heard her give to Joe."

Martin replied, "Quite the contrary. Context is everything. Usually, she is quite an inspirational teacher. Her students all have an excellent grasp of the curriculum through her differentiated teaching and learning activities."

Martin continued, "She is also strategic in the planning and execution of her lessons. She focuses on intent, impact and implementation. This is evident when learners are quizzed about their learning journey, the information they can recall, as well as, the results obtained. Her lessons are also fantastic. She begins every lesson with exciting starter activities which heightens her students' interest and engagement prior to diving deep into the topic.

Mrs. Fanny also has a way of making her students feel valued and it improves their success rate," Martin continued. "I am pretty sure Joe still feels valued and I hope that that one incident won't put him off. They know that Mrs. Fanny is demanding due to her high expectations of them. It is no wonder her students always do well in her subject and because of that, they can't wait to know their scores, hence they keep harassing her for answers."

I turned to Martin and asked, "How do you know that she does all those things you have mentioned Martin?"

Martin replied, "You too will soon find out for yourself. Every term, your manager sends around the list she prepares for us to peer observe each other. Also, remember the learning walks that senior management does during our lessons and the weekly feedback they give. I know our department generally performs well, and that we are all doing a great job, but Mrs Fanny's lessons are consistent and exceptional, in my opinion. I do enjoy doing peer observations with her."

Did you know that her students actually get upset when they arrive late to her lessons? Yes, they do. That is because they don't want to miss anything. However, having said that, I think she might have been a bit insensitive today, but who doesn't get it wrong sometimes, especially under pressure?"

Martin continued; Mrs. Fanny has set a precedent. Sometimes, I don't know whether she is just well organised or she has a competitive spirit, but regardless, she always gives prompt feedback ahead of us all. Maybe something went wrong this time and she found herself under pressure, so she snapped. She is never usually like that. I can tell you; they love her. Joe wouldn't have approached her if he felt she wouldn't entertain him. She is also well learned, so students access her like a library because she always has an informed answer to give even outside of her subject area.

Allison continued, "Elsie, I listened to Martin but I was still shocked by Mrs. Fanny's response and reaction to poor Joe. I told him straight that I didn't care how great a teacher she is, and that if one had to choose, empathy would always triumph over intellectuality. Mrs. Fanny's attitude to Joe didn't show that she cared. She might have cared about her students' intellectual needs, but what about their social and emotional wellbeing?

As one of the more disciplined students, it was just unfortunate for Joe. He didn't deserve such tongue-lashing. Poor Joe's self-esteem must have been shattered, especially with all of us in the staffroom listening in. I wasn't impressed at all.

I went on to tell Martin that while I was still practicing law, we had to be professional and we had a duty to care for all our clients. Teaching shouldn't be different. I believe, as teachers, we have to be always mindful of our responses. Then I asked him to answer me honestly. "Do you think that conversation left Joe feeling valued? As the scripture says,

> *"Thoughtless words can wound as deeply as any sword, but wisely spoken words can heal." (Proverbs 12:18 GNT)*

Just a plain, honest response would have alleviated the situation instead. Nevertheless, don't get me wrong, we all get it wrong sometimes. I made my own mistakes too, especially when dealing with difficult clients during my law career, and I had to apologise to them. To err is human, after all.

Martin seemed less unmoved by my opinion, he only shrugged and said, "Allison, the dynamics in teaching change from moment to moment, day to day and year to year. If you are in it long enough like Mrs. Fanny or even me, you would understand. I will give you some time to adjust. I have been a full-time teacher for twenty-three years. But now, I am slowly working my way out. As soon as my business is up and running, I am gone. Don't get me wrong. It is a noble profession with a lot of intrinsic rewards especially when you see your students succeed, but increasingly, there is too much pressure and almost no work-life balance. Most of our time is spent at work, and we also take work home both physically and emotionally. Even if you work online, there is no escape route. It's a vicious cycle."

In teaching, one has to continually develop new skill sets to keep up with the ever-changing curriculum demands, and I am not prepared to do that any longer. That is why I am trying to diversify my portfolio and invest in other things in the meantime. Who knows, my second business might be the one that launches me into my destiny. The Great Book of Instruction states:

> *"Send your grain across the seas, and in time,*
> *profits will flow back to you.*
> *But divide your investments among many places, for*

He continued, "I personally believe one has to be called and be graced to teach, else you will not have the passion to endure when the going gets tough. That is why in life, one needs to have a plan. A realistic plan with SMART goals and also to work towards accomplishing them. Sure, there would be times when things might not go as intended, but having a plan would give you something to focus your attention and energy on. Plans also help you to measure your progress over time and to recalibrate, if you veer off track.

"It's like running a restaurant business," he said. "In order to stay ahead of competitors, you have to keep diversifying your menu by adding new dishes regularly. This gives customers variety and also attracts new ones. In doing so, it will continue to boost sales and hopefully keep the business viable in the future.

Martin went on to say, "Personally, I have a plan." He said he knew I was still fairly young and full of enthusiasm for life, but then he asked, "do you have a plan? The question caught me unaware, Elsie. It was like a jolt to my system. I felt this sudden emptiness, like I'd been sailing along with no real direction, just drifting. Truly, I didn't have a plan. I hadn't even thought about it in those terms.

As if sensing my uncertainty, he said, "You need one for your life, dear. That's the only way you are going to be able to know how well you are doing, and whether you are achieving your objectives. I wish someone had informed me like this when I was as young as you are, Allison. Maybe I would have avoided the pain of making certain mistakes."

I didn't know how to respond to him, and he continued, "Again, as an older colleague and friend, I ask once again, do you have a plan for your life, Allison? What if, like law, you suddenly don't like teaching? What if something should happen to you or your family in the future? What will you do? You also need to plan your finances. Teaching is hard enough. You cannot afford to waste that hard-earned cash. Sometimes we bleed in our hearts to earn our salaries, given the abuse we often get from dissident students, and recently, their number keeps increasing. I could hear the frustration in his voice, and quite truthfully, teaching could be draining, physically and emotionally. He concluded: you need to think on these things Allison. Save for a rainy day. Always have something to call your own. Always have a back-up plan. Don't let life surprise you in ways that could be avoided.

Allison paused for some minutes, her voice taking on a more reflective tone. "For some reason, Martin couldn't stop speaking and I couldn't stop listening to him either. I didn't open up to him about my personal life as it was still early days into the job and I wasn't quite ready to share everything, but I was intrigued by his counsel. My parents taught me to listen to and respect my elders, so I didn't mind his advice.

Martin continued, his voice soft but firm, I don't know your situation, Allison, but in my own case, even though my parents are aged, I never think of relying on my family's inheritance. I don't think too much about it either because what I achieve on my own is mine and none of my siblings can cause a fuss with me over it. His eyes seemed to search mine as he said, "I don't know why and it's weird, I don't mean to intrude, but I just feel compelled to talk to you about this. Please don't let what I am saying come back to haunt you later, Allison. I hope it never does. I counsel a number of young individuals in my part-time voluntary role at a charity and I like to see young individuals thrive. I guess this zeal stemmed from my experience working with charities over the years, giving young individuals the drive and advice they need to maximise their potential.

Allison gave Elsie a long stare, "Elsie, after Martin finished speaking, I was puzzled. I said to myself, 'Aw! That's where his compulsion to speak to me came from, from his part-time counselling role.' However, that evening, I went home with mixed feelings. Whilst listening to Martin, I was both challenged and inspired. His words pierced my heart like a dagger, and a sudden fear enveloped me. It felt as if it was an angel that was warning me ahead of things to come. It felt prophetic. I wondered if I had appeared wasteful or irresponsible, and that's why he had to speak to me the way he did; but I guessed I needed it at the time because I was certainly too carefree.

Lately, after all those years, I have been reflecting and it was as if Martin foresaw my downfall because, now, I have absolutely nothing —no savings whatsoever. I am broke, bankrupt and still don't even have a plan in place as yet. I feel like the prodigal son. The only difference is, I have no father's home to return to. It feels rather strange, awful and pathetic but that's the reality of my life right now. Martin was right. "Don't rely on family inheritance, have your own." Our family inheritance is lost in my dad's head ever since he developed Huntington's disease. He was the accountant and

CEO of our family fortune. Now, he doesn't even know himself.

Allison continued, her voice tinged with frustration, "Although I am not proud of it, I must admit that I have 'hit rock bottom' and it currently feels like hell. It feels hopeless, like a person who has driven into a cul-de-sac and the only way out is to turn around, but to make matters worse, my vehicle is stuck. It has run out of petrol and hit the curb. So, without help, I cannot even move. I want to turn things around right now, but I don't know how.

At rock bottom, the only consolation is that there is no further to go except to arise and get out of the situation, out of the mess. That's what has been giving me hope and has kept me looking up from the valley each day. I have fallen so low - emotionally, financially, relationally, spiritually and even in my ability to communicate at times. Even the sparkling rays of sunlight at times seemed dim amidst the dense fog that's trying to block my view from looking and getting up.

Allison continued, with a wry smile, "A few days ago, it was that sunlight that began to slowly pierce through my gloom giving me a sliver of hope to rise and try again. One of the rays of that sunlight is you, Elsie. I met you amidst the gloom that day in the café and God's light has been shining through you to encourage me. Since then, I have started to feel a glimmer of hope once again.

Allison smiled softly at Elsie's words, feeling a warmth spread through her and said, "Aw Allison! We give God all the glory. We all need people so that, if we meet misfortune, lose our way, err or even fall, they can be the hands and feet of God to put us back on the right path.

Allison with a thoughtful look on her face sighed as she said, "Life is a mystery. I did have a lot of friends around me at university, but I never thought I would be in a position where I would really need anyone. I don't mean to sound arrogant or invincible, but I thought I had it all together. Now, I have come to realise that no one is infallible.

Elsie with a broad and warm smile said, "Of course, Allison. I cannot forget you. I believe the way we treat others always leaves them with an unforgettable experience, whether good or bad. My experience with you Allison has been amazing. It is one that I will forever treasure.

At university, you were like an angel to us. You touched our lives in very meaningful ways. The material things you gave to us might have long disappeared but we all cannot forget how you made us feel. You made us feel special, Allison. And that is one of the unique things about relationships in general. One might not always be able to give people everything they need, but they will stay in a relationship with you if you value them, and make them feel special. Showing love, respect, empathy and being honest is part of what makes someone feel valued."

Elsie continued, "I presume a number of things have happened or gone wrong in your life Allison, and you felt the impact so massively because you have been on your own all this time. That's why the scripture says, *"Two people are better off than one, for they can help each other succeed. If one person falls, the other can reach out and help. But someone who falls alone is in real trouble." (Ecclesiastes 4:9-10 NLT)*

"I am glad we find each other again, Allison, and I do hope I can help to mitigate some of the impact of your 'fall.' I am also not infallible myself and who knows? You might one day be the one to help me in ways that I cannot help myself.

Allison said, "Prior to meeting you Elsie, as you can see, I had fallen alone and have been in real trouble. You have been a God-send in that café that day and ever since.

Elsie was touched. "Aw Allison! I am hoping that I can do more for you as we journey together now. Did you know that everyone has a guardian angel and that they are always on assignment, ready to help recalibrate anyone who has strayed or suffered misfortune? I believe we were divinely re-connected that day in the café.

Allison nodded, her voice resolute, "Yes, I never gave up hope. Despite all the mishaps and insults I experienced at the café, I kept going back. It was as if destiny was calling me. I just had that compelling feeling to keep going back to that café. I could hear the inner voice always saying to me, 'Keep visiting a bit longer.' Now I realise that it was in order to get connected to you. You are one of my destiny helpers, Elsie."

Elsie with eyes full of understanding and compassion replied, "Thanks Allison. I want you to get up out of that valley of despair you described earlier. Don't sit there, walk through it. Like the Psalmist says, 'Yea, though I walk through the valley of the shadow of death, I will fear no evil.' (Psalms 23:4 KJV). I know sometimes life can hit us with crippling blows, but you don't have to be crippled or remain crippled by them. You can get back up. You can walk again or even fly too.

Allison went on, "As I continue to reflect, I remember the scripture verse that says, *"Don't forget to be kind to strangers, for some who have done this have entertained angels without realizing it! (Hebrews 12:12 Living Bible).* Looking back on my conversation with Martin, I now realise that I was entertaining an angel unaware. I wished I had heeded his instructions."

"Martin was an angel in disguise. I have been taking time out to reflect on my life lately. What he said to me then, was correct. At the time, I didn't have a plan. I was 29 years old, young, and I felt invincible as everything was running smoothly. I had brushed aside his words, thinking that I had my parents' fortune to inherit, which would serve as a security, being an only child. Up till now, I still haven't managed to put a plan together. I guess that helps to explain the situation I am in now. And now I know this saying to be very true: *"people don't plan to fail, but they fail to plan."*

Since listening to Martin and reflecting on my brief teaching career, I've found myself feeling more empathy for Mrs Fanny than I ever imagined I could. Thinking about it now, Mrs. Fanny's attitude towards Joe that day might have been a direct result of the workload pressure that teachers face daily. Of course, that doesn't justify being harsh to students.

On the surface, teaching is perceived to be a profession where one gets a lot of free time to relax and jet off to anywhere on the planet during the holidays. At least, that's the common perception, right? I said, raising an eyebrow, thinking about how most people saw it. Elsie chuckled, but didn't give any verbal answer.

So, Allison continued, "However, now I'm beginning to understand the vicious cycle of workload that teachers have to endure. It's exhausting, almost inescapable. The only solution to it is to do as Mrs. Fanny did, to mark as soon as you receive the scripts. But honestly, where is the time to do that?

Teachers usually have a full-time table, juggling a full schedule of lessons alongside countless number of meetings, and Continuing Professional Development (CPD) training to attend. This leaves little room during work hours to mark, if you don't want to take a lot of it home. Then there are department meetings and admin duties. Teachers are also basically on call to attend to students' affairs anytime throughout the day even during non-contact time. Therefore, one has to learn how to be emotionally intelligent in managing interruptions to one's daily tasks and not get flustered and frustrated over it.

I took a deep breath, feeling the weight of it all. "Consequently, the mental stress and strain of the day-to-day job can impair a teacher's judgement and ability to remain calm and collected under pressure. I therefore concluded that teaching is not for the faint-hearted. I believe one has to be called to the profession or like it well enough to remain in it. The planning, delivery, marking, meeting external examination board deadlines for coursework, coupled with preparing students for internal and external examinations, external government inspection, and then all the pastoral care.

Not to mention attending Staff and Parents' meetings along with the burden of admin.

Elsie shook her head. "It's a lot. I don't know how anyone keeps up with all of that."

"Painfully, it's usually the teacher who gets blamed if students are not attending and achieving," I said, shaking my head. "It seems to be a never-ending cycle and it can take a toll on the teachers' health and well-being over time. Even in the short-term, some teachers' health is affected depending on the institution, its management, ethos and what support it has in place for both staff and students." Elsie nodded quietly in agreement.

"Regarding the enviable holidays, thinking about it is like adding salt to a wound," I said, my voice tinged with bitterness. "It may provide some relief but the process of getting there is still very painful. Teachers' holidays are set by the government so they can only jet out of the country during half-term, Christmas, Easter and summer breaks. And of course, the airline industry has smartly set those times as their peak season for travelling which means ticket prices are sky-high. Resultantly, it can cost "an arm and a leg" for many teachers with families thereby creating additional stress that they are trying to escape and get relief from.".

"How Mrs. Fanny managed to cope for 30 years and still going strong, was in itself amazing and commendable. I said, my voice full of awe. "One has to be wired for teaching to remain in it that long." So, I asked myself, "Was this the right route for me?" At least, Martin had a plan. However, the teaching profession like many others, has an inbuilt training mechanism to enable teachers to continue to develop and to acquire new skills sets to manage the curriculum and students' behaviour. And that's not just for the teacher's benefit, it also adds value to the students in terms of achievement, retention and even their destination after completing their studies.

"I didn't think I was good at planning," I said, shaking my head. "And honestly, I never really tried to stick to a plan. I don't mean lesson planning but planning my own life. I'd rather let things flow as I go along, regardless of what anyone thinks. To me, that's an adventure in itself, or so I thought. I had hoped things would work out for me by operating that way but it didn't. I have now come to realise that, that's a frivolous way to live one's life."

I paused, my gaze dropping for a moment before continuing, my voice laced with regret "I was too carefree and too strong headed to listen to Martin or even to my parents. This was because I had my thoughts set on my parents' fortune, being their only child. Who wouldn't think that way when they have no other siblings to contend with? Actually, back then, I thought it was a great plan, foolish as it might have seemed now. It was my back-up plan, but of course, it failed."

> *What do you do when your plans fail to materialise?*

6

CONCERN FOR ALLISON

At times, it seems as if one has to 'go through' in order to 'get through' life. At other times, life feels like a game of snake and ladder. You work hard trying to reach the apex, carefully navigating all the snake bites and downward spirals of the ladder in order to get there. Suddenly, whilst the end is in view, you get stung by a huge snake which forces you to start all over again. I am sure we are not alone in this struggle. The good thing is that those same ladders that took us down, are still there to help us climb back up again, only if we have the courage to keep trying.

As I was thinking about it, I got carried away as I listened to Allison trying to update me on the missing years. She had so much to say, and things seemed to be going so well until... Then I realised I had to do school runs. The school had contacted me earlier to collect the twins. They were closing the school earlier than usual that evening due to an important call, followed by an emergency staff meeting. It turned out to be about an imminent visit from the government inspection team. Most educational institutions usually get flustered about news like that, and they were no exception. I had just thirty minutes to collect the children.

I also wanted to continue hearing Allison's story, but I thought it was an opportunity for her to go home and soak her wounds in a warm bath with sea salt and Manuka honey. The Manuka honey, with its potent healing properties, would be perfect for the bruises she had sustained when she fell in the road.

The school was only within five to ten minutes' walk. From a distance, we could hear the buzz of noise from the children as they emerged through the school gate. It reminded me of a time when Gina and some of her friends were walking through a thick woodland with low hanging branches. Gina's hair accidentally got tangled into one of the branches, and in trying to free herself, she unknowingly upset a beehive. They all had to run for their lives.

As you cannot differentiate a single bee in the distance from all the other bees, I couldn't recognise Vin and Vanessa in their school uniforms amongst the other children. But as I got closer, I could hear two distinctive little voices racing towards us and shouting excitedly, "Mum, Mum, Mum, you are eaaaarly!" They both jumped up on me and I could tell which one had eaten and which still had their packed lunch intact. Then Vin pointed and asked, "Who is that mum?" "Err! Her dress is ugly" he added. I quickly covered his mouth as if I was removing some particles of food. Then I enquired from him what he had eaten. I then politely smiled at Allison and said, "Don't mind him. They don't understand fabric prints."

As we carried on walking, I told Allison that they were practicing for the upcoming pantomime and learning how to dramatize events. It's all part of their little acting roles, I explained, referring to the rude comment Vin had made earlier. Of course, Allison isn't silly and she understood the psychology and curiosity of little children. Soon after, Allison said goodbye as we crossed the road. By then, I had forgotten to give her the dollar she had asked for earlier in the café and she didn't remind me. I guess being in my company was slowly restoring her dignity and she felt she couldn't ask me again, or maybe the desire for food had been satisfied as we kept eating between intervals. Whatever the reason, I wasn't too bothered. We had planned on seeing each other the following Saturday for a volunteer event at a local charity.

After tucking the children into bed, I had mixed emotions. I was thinking about Allison's social and emotional well-being, and where she was going to spend the night, though she didn't raise it as a concern. I didn't know whether she had somewhere to stay. I wanted to establish all the facts, but I realised it might take some time. Still, I had huge concerns for her.

Given what she had said earlier, I might be the only one she knows that could be of any assistance to her. Metaphorically, I wanted to take her out of the vicious ocean of life that was infested with sharks, killer whales and other cannibal fishes and transfer her to a pond where she could be nurtured and better cared for. Then, when she was strong enough to contend with the elements, she would be released back into the ocean. So far, it seemed like teaching had left an indelible print on her mind, as she shared her experience with great thoughtfulness.

Although curious, my intention was not only to hear Allison's story or to give her a dollar. Even though I was still trying to understand her lifestyle, I realised that she needed much more than money. However, I didn't want to give her money to spend on the wrong things. I didn't know if at that point, she was taking hard substances, gambling or sleeping rough or whether any of those things were part of her. I didn't have all the facts yet, but regardless, I wanted to offer her tangible help. The kind of help that would bring real solution to her life, including shelter and medical check-ups, even if it meant paying for her to go to a rehabilitation centre. I also wanted her to get back into full-time employment to help restore her dignity and self-esteem. I was concerned about her well-being. In the process, I also intended to encourage her to have a plan for her life this time around, and to stick to it as much as possible.

I wanted her to plan the change she wanted to see, and to become that change. However, it was evident that she was still focused on survival. So, before that could happen, her basic needs of food, shelter, clothing, finances and safety needed to be taken care of. Then she could move on to getting back into the job market, rebuilding her circle of friends, and eventually starting to date again.

So far, I believed Allison had said enough, and my heart was already moved with compassion to act, although unknown to her. Sometimes, one doesn't have to say much especially when the situation is already visible and obvious. Then I remembered the scripture that says,

> *"Suppose you see a brother or sister who has no food or clothing, and you say, "Good-bye and have a good day; stay warm and eat well"—but then you don't give that person any food or clothing. What good does that do? (James 2:15-16NLT).*

Technically it felt like that was what I was doing on the surface, but in reality, I was working on meeting her needs.

Then, as I continued reading, I came across this other scripture, and I felt rather guilty knowing that I was living in comfort and safety, unlike Allison. It read as follows:

> *"If you can help your neighbour now, don't say,*
> *"Come back tomorrow, and then I'll help you."*
> *(Proverbs 3:28 NLT).*

That's what I actually did. I planned on meeting up with her instead of trying to find a way to make things happen for her that day. Maybe it was easier said than done, because some help is not as instantaneous given the processes involved. However, there are times when some needs are so urgent that they should be responded to immediately. I believe, if Allison had told me that she didn't have anywhere to sleep that night, who knows, I would have taken her home with me and explained to my family later, or paid for lodging for her.

As a Sunday school teacher, it was only a few weeks prior to seeing Allison that I was discussing this text with the class:

> *"For I was hungry, and you fed me. I was thirsty, and you gave me a drink. I was a stranger, and you invited me into your home. I was naked, and you gave me clothing. I was sick, and you cared for me. I was in prison, and you visited me." (Matthew 25:35-36 NLT).*

Love is not merely words. It is doing practical things to help humanity, especially those who are not in a position to help themselves at the time. Sometimes, people just need a push-start, like that of a stalled car, to get back on the road again and Allison was one such person.

Suddenly, the house phone rang and interrupted my thoughts. I muttered to myself, "Who is it now?" I was already feeling mentally exhausted from thinking a lot about Allison. The last thing I wanted was a phone conversation. I just wanted to relax longer in the warm vanilla and mint fragrance steamed bath after seeing my children off to bed. My husband, Les, ran to the bathroom door, covering the phone with his palm and in an excited tone, said, "Darling Elsie! It's your call."

I sighed in hesitation, then signalled for him to find out who it was. It was Dr Carey from Charity Odyssey. "Poor old man," I thought. "If I were a retired surgeon like him, I would be in Hawaii, enjoying the beautiful islands and sunbathing on the deck of a luxury yacht." But not Dr Carey. He was a retired surgeon who still found time to serve his community. He had opened a non-profit agency to help 'battered people' find their way back to wholeness through counselling and employment, so that their dignity could be restored. Every time I think of the word 'battered', I am forced to reflect on the advert for poor Rocky, the dog who was beaten, battered, shot and left for dead. It seemed that's what life has done to too many people including Allison.

"What does he want now?" I sighed in silence. "Honey, please tell him I'll return his call."

Immediately, I heard a voice in my head, it said, "Elsie, those who truly love, truly care." I was speechless, I quickly dried myself and rushed out of the tub.

Those who truly love, truly care.

7

A CATCH-UP MEETING

I couldn't wait to see Allison again, and I wondered which was more urgent: returning Dr Carey's call about hiring a carer for my mother-in-law, Mama Tamer; or turning up to see Allison? With not much time left, I chose the latter.

I arrived at the local charity as arranged, parked my yellow jeep and stayed inside, listening to music. I still hadn't eaten much or slept well since, because Allison's situation haunted me. Just then, *Hit 2 radio* began playing the song "Amazing Grace" and immediately, Allison's life flashed before me like a movie. I sobbed as I heard the verse:

> *Through many dangers, toils, and snares*
> *I have already come*
> *This grace that brought me safe thus far*
> *And grace will lead me home.*

With tearful eyes, I looked up and there through the window in the thick fog, I saw the silhouette of a person coming towards me. The walking reminded me of Allison when we were at university —the gait, the confidence, the posture. But shortly after, I realised it wasn't her. The person then got into a blue mini and drove off. A few more people passed by, and I tried to see if Allison was among them. This time, I was certain that it was her when I saw the limp. It felt like she was coming home. Coming home after many years of dangers, toil and snares.

And there she was, walking towards the carpark on the opposite side of the charity building. She looked stunningly elegant in her long green dress cinched with gold belt and a pair of flat orange ballet shoes, with matching earrings and a handbag. Her belt and shoes glittered in the thick fog, and her limp was less obvious due to her long attire.

I was distracted from the song as I started to watch Allison's every step as she approached my yellow jeep. Memories of our brief time reconnecting flooded my mind, and I reflected on the excerpts and incidents she had shared about her life.

As I continued to watch her walking towards the car park, a few thoughts rushed through my mind, and I began to ask myself some rhetorical questions. "What if you were walking in a great city such as London or New York and you looked down on the street and suddenly saw a torn and slightly crushed fifty-pound note, or a one-hundred-dollar bill in US currency? What would you do? Would you turn a blind eye or would you pick it up?" I believe that even if you were loaded with cash, you wouldn't think twice. You would still pick it up.

However, regardless of the decision made, do you think that fifty-pound note or one-hundred-dollar bill would be of any less value because of where it was found? Would its value diminish because it was dirty, torn and slightly crushed?

"No!" I said to myself. "Not at all."

Immediately, I realised that I was answering my own thoughts. Then it struck me: whether the note was dirty, torn or crushed, as long as its serial number and other features were still intact, that note would still be a legal tender. Any bank would accept it because the note hasn't lost its value, even though it had been mismanaged.

As Allison drew closer, I thought to myself, "You might have been mismanaged like that bank note, but you haven't lost your value. You might have lost a number of things in your life, but you haven't lost your value. You might have lost your father, your husband, your home, your job, your money, your friends, your dignity and your self-esteem, but you haven't lost your value.

Like that bank note, you still have your serial number and other defining features intact. You are still the Allison we knew at university — despite the struggles, the hardship, the limp and the disappearance of material wealth. Most importantly, you haven't lost your mind. That means you can recreate your life through positive affirmation and purposeful actions. You are going to recover all, and exceed even your own expectations!"

Then my mind continued to race with more thoughts, and I began to think: Your tomorrow is going to be greater than your yesterday. You matter to us. You matter to someone out there in the world, waiting to show you love and to give you the help you need to get back on track again. But most importantly, you matter to God. God will mobilise people and things in your environment to favour and help you.

God is the One who is capable of healing broken hearts, mending shattered thoughts, restoring broken dreams, repairing broken homes and fixing lives that have been torn apart. He is the great Carpenter, the Master Builder and

Maker. He is the Great Mr. Fix- It, the Master Potter. No job is too difficult for him to design, redesign or repair.

God is amazing. At times, He will do a new thing in your life and then at other times, he just makes all things new. (Isaiah 43:19; Revelation 21:5). God cannot run out of options and He cannot err or fail. There is no searching of His understanding.

Like a Potter, sometimes the jar doesn't meet expectations, and he would crush it and start again. God made you a masterpiece. If you are not at your best right now, and have fallen short of his expectations, could it be that, like the potter, He is taking you through the crushing process? Always remember, God expects nothing but the best from you. So, don't cry, and don't be alarmed. The finished product is what matters. Look at the message God gave to the prophet in the scriptures below:

> '*The* L*ORD* *gave another message to Jeremiah. He said, "Go down to the potter's shop, and I will speak to you there." So, I did as he told me and found the potter working at his wheel. But the jar he was making did not turn out as he had hoped, so he crushed it into a lump of clay again and started over. Then the* L*ORD* *gave me this message: "O Israel, can I not do to you as this potter has done to his clay? As the clay is in the potter's hand, so are you in my hand." (Jeremiah 18:1-6 NLT)*

So, don't run away from hardship, it could be part of the process. You are in the Potter's hand. It will turn out to your advantage.

When we find that our 'jars' have become marred by the adversities of life, we need to place ourselves again into the Potter's hand and allow him to put us back together because none of us is infallible. Sometimes we might feel that our lives have fallen out of shape or even shattered into pieces. However, no matter how shapeless, hopeless and scattered those pieces of our lives are, God, the Great Potter, knows where each piece is, and He is more than capable of putting our lives back together again and making us new, if we would believe and trust him.

If you feel that this has resonated with you or someone you know, pause and say this prayer:

> *Father, in the name of Jesus, you have made me into your image and likeness but I didn't turn out as you purposed. I fell short of your glory. I am now in your hands as a jar is in the potter's hand. Make me over. Make me new. Reshape and redecorate me so that I can fulfil the purpose for which You have created me and enjoy life to its fullest. Amen.*

God has us in the palm of His hands. He also knows about our situations. He knows the storms that have brought devastations to our lives.

God will never turn away anyone who genuinely comes to Him. He is always available, willing and able to help us in times of need.

Sometimes the challenges of life can get us weary and cause us to want to give up. Regardless of the situation you find yourself in, God will answer, whether you bring the issues directly to Him or through someone else who seeks Him on your behalf. Whichever way, He will be at work in your situation. He restores, refreshes and renews, so don't give up.

We should always remember that *our value is not in what we own, but to whom we belong.* We belong to God, our Creator. The One who owns all things.

As Allison came through the gate, I opened the car door and beckoned for her to come over. We still had 15 minutes before the start of the charity event.

In an upbeat tone and a wide smile, I said to Allison, "Girl, you look great! It's a pleasure seeing you again! "Give me a high five!"

We touched hands and embraced each other.

With a playful grin, I turned to Allison. "Allie, do you have a date later?"

Allison blushed then said, "I wish." She glanced down at her outfit and added with a soft laugh, "I bought this dress on my way back from Sydney, way back in those days at university. I don't even know if I am well coordinated. Am I?"

With an encouraging grin, I said, "Yes, of course!" "Girl, you rock!"

"Memories of our university days flashed through my mind as you entered the car park."

Allison blushed once again. "Now you made me feel conscious that I haven't even gained any weight since. I used to wear this dress without a belt."

Allison had dressed so elegantly and her perfume was so refreshing yet subtle, it instantly enhanced the atmosphere within the car.

Allison sighed, her tone earnest. "Right now, my mind is on getting back to work, Elsie. I wish I were going to a job interview. I am desperate to work. Jobs seem to be as scarce as water in the Sahara Desert these days. I wish I was still teaching or practicing law, as stressful as it was back then.

Allison seemed eager to unburden herself and with a sudden shift in tone, she changed the subject to the topic I had been waiting all along to hear.

Allison looked at me thoughtfully, her voice carrying a tinge of weariness. "Frankie, my estranged husband, was an opportunist. He enjoyed the lavish lifestyle- jetting off with me every school holiday, and going to tournaments or to any sporting event he chose. You see, my husband changed cars through our family's joint business twice every year with all-expense paid. He became arrogant, wasteful and complacent. One moment he would be driving an ordinary Mercedes, but as summer approaches, he wanted something sportier, so he would ask for a sports model, and my parents, as indulgent as ever, made his wishes their command. No wonder he didn't want a permanent job. He opted for contract work because he liked to receive gross income. It fed his ego it seemed. In a regular job, he would be taxed at the source but he chose to take his salary in contractual terms through his own company so that he can manage his own tax, or rather, leave it to his accountant parent to handle. In that way, he likes to see the lump sum coming in, but managing it wisely was another issue. And when construction slowed down during off-seasons, he would sometimes be out of work for up to six months.

One day I was reflecting on Frankie's job situation and received an insight about two rivers. It was like an intuition. Probably it's because I had seen similar rivers when I was growing up as a child. The insight from them struck me and I thought to share it with him.

I looked at him thoughtfully. "Frankie, I have a puzzle for you to solve".

Frankie smirked with confidence "Where is it? Bring it on."

I continued calmly. "There were two farming villages in a rural area and their survival depended on the river that runs through them. One village, Evergreen, had a single river that faithfully served it over the years without fail. It is not the most powerfully flowing river, but its water was always constant. It never ceased to flow, so the villagers and their vegetation were always watered. A variety of fishes also thrived in that river including catfish, trout and crayfish. So, the villagers not only enjoyed its water supply, they also depended on it for a major source of their protein. As a result, it attracted the local fishermen and it provided much fun as well for children trying to catch crayfish.

Some of the youths often went for a swim and sometimes had little impromptu fishing and swimming competitions. Sometimes they would sell the fishes they caught or roast them on the river bank.

All this time Frankie listened intently. He probably wondered what I was getting up to. Then I continued,

The second village, Savage, also had a river which served the entire community and its vegetation. The flow of this river was five times more powerful than that of Evergreen. When it flowed, the current was so powerful, it took everything in its path including humans and livestock. Even experienced fishermen had to think twice before entering it. But, the trouble with this river was, it didn't flow constantly. It was unpredictable, and it sometimes flowed unexpectedly even in the absence of heavy rains.

At other times, the community would experience long dry periods leading to severe droughts. There was also no bridge at some section where this river ran, so children and others would often forget that a river existed there and would play in the river bed. The villagers, too, used its path as a normal crossing for their livestock and everyday activities. Oftentimes, motorbikes and even four-wheel drive vehicles would cross its rugged terrain. Then suddenly, without warning, the river would come crashing like a Tsunami, bursting its banks, rushing through the village and taking almost everything and everyone in its path by surprise.

Children using it as a shortcut from school or playing in its path often got caught by surprise and were violently swept away, along with many farmers and their livestock. The flow is so rapid that the villagers have no time to act in response and get out of its path. Then, after a couple of days, its water would recede until months later or whenever a heavy rain descends again.

Unlike Evergreen that always had fish, the current from Savage usually carries a lot of fishes and huge ones too, but after it stopped flowing, everything would perish. The fishes would lie fluttering around on the ground until people picked them up or they just lay there until they "ran out of oxygen. It was like a mystical river.

After relating the two accounts to Frankie, I turned to him and asked him which of the two rivers was better? He said to me, "Obviously, River Evergreen." I then said to him, "Think of the rivers as two different sources of employment and re-evaluate your job situation." He replied, "Of late, I have been thinking about it." Frankie always turned down permanent posts thinking the salary wasn't good enough. However, in the long-term, he had come to realise that permanent jobs are much better as it gives stability in terms of income flow. He told me he would be seeking permanent employment from then onwards. Then he turned and said to me, "Allie, no wonder you studied law. You are a very insightful person, a real brainbox indeed." I smiled and thought to myself, probably if I were, I wouldn't have been with you, but I allowed sleeping dogs to lie.

Frankie had dual personalities – an angel to my parents but a hooligan at sporting events and even to me at home. Since he was so wonderful to my parents, he became the son they wanted but didn't have. When he wasn't working, the few hours he spent indoors was taken up by watching rugby, football, motor racing or even online betting. Other times, especially when it was nearing the time to change his car again, he would hang out with my parents, spending almost every weekend with them.

Once at a football match, there was an altercation between him and another person from his opponent's side. It was one of those situations that could have been avoided, yet it escalated so quickly. The event is still vivid in my mind:

We were at the match when suddenly Frankie glared at Floyd, a spectator in his Leeward side Jersey. "YOW MATE! Why have you tattooed my wife's name on your arm?" "That's my wife's name – Allie." "Are you thinking of embracing her into your arms at some point, mate?"

He was obviously trying to start an altercation with the young man. I thought maybe he had a few drinks at home before leaving, as this was becoming his custom.

Frankie should have known that the name 'Allie' is fairly popular, and that a tattoo was a common and personal matter. It could have been the man's child or lover's name. As a matter of fact, nobody owns a particular name. Names are not patented.

Floyd, the Leeward side spectator, ignored Frankie and kept chatting with his friend as if nothing had happened.

Frankie turned pink, his face contorted with anger. He screamed and shouted "SO, YOU ARE IGNORING ME, EH!"

Then, shaking his head from side to side and with raised eyebrows and increased volume, he shouted, "YOU ARE IGNORING MEEEH! Do you know who I am? DO YOU KNOW WHO I AM?"

At this point, I concluded that he was intoxicated.

Floyd's friend shouted over, his voice loud and mocking "YES! We know who you are. A STOW-AWAY. AN ALIEN. A

LOSER FROM MARS! Yes! AN IDIOT. AN IGNORANT LOSER! Go back to the galaxies, LOSEEEERR! No wonder you are supporting Fuzzy side. YOU FUZZ! You must be made from FUR."

At this point, other Leeward side spectators joined in shouting, "LET'S BLOW HIM BACK TO MARS!"

Everyone chuckled and chanted, "MARS! MARS! FUZZ! FUZZ!" "You loser team FUZ!" My stomach tightened with embarrassment as the crowd erupted in laughter.

Then suddenly some of the young spectators began to blow bubbles in the air as if it was planned, and the banter intensified as the bubbles floated into the air.

They chuckled again and pointed to the sky: "THERE HE IS IN THAT BUBBLE GOING BACK TO MARS."

Laughter and boos erupted even louder.

The Leeward side spectators continued. "Let's throw some hot tea on him later. Roast him for barbeque and feed him to the pigs on Uncle Mac's farm," they teased. "YOU BIG HEAD! No! YOU PIG HEAD! Go back to mars! No! Jupiter instead." And they blew even more bubbles. Then laughter and boos erupted again.

I immediately feared for Frankie, because I could see that he was in real trouble. Were they going to mob him later? I didn't intervene, though, because I was too scared. I was scared that he would immediately turn on me there and then, or wait to have live wrestling and kickboxing later when we got home.

I thought he brought it on himself, so he had no one to blame but himself. It was hilarious, and I had no empathy for him, because it was an attack born out of his own provocation.

The commentator's voice boomed across the stadium, "And here comes Des, Des passes to Truan, Truan to Pano. Pano is looking for Mus. And here comes Mus! Mus took a long shot. He took a long shot!"

Frankie, still fuming, shot back, "So your friends are laughing at me eh!"

With that, he opened the can of beer he had tucked under his seat and threw it into the crowd, in the direction of the laughter and boos.

The Leeward side spectators stood up screaming in shock.

At first, I wasn't sure if the spectators were reacting to the spray from the can of beer or to the long ball being aimed at the net, so I quickly dashed towards the rest room area for cover.

The Commentator shouted, "And he scored! Mus scored! Mus scored! What an incredible goal! What an incredible goal from such a long ball!"

The Leeward side Players jumped on Mus then lifted and threw him into the air in excitement. It was his first goal of the season. They had advanced to the semi-final.

The Leeward side spectators were still on their feet in jubilation, jumping up and down, dancing, screaming, shouting, flying their flags and chanting.

It appeared like the roof of the stadium was suddenly lifted. The atmosphere was electrifying indeed!

The Commentator continued. "Mus took the long ball and landed it at the back of the net. Brilliant! Brilliant indeed! Not an everyday occurrence! The goal keeper had no chance! No chance whatsoever!"

The Leeward side spectators, still standing, shouted, "LEEWARD! AWARD! LEEWARD! AWARD! Mus! Mus!"

Elsie, I froze in the excitement all around me. I stood half way between going to the restroom and watching the game. At one point, I forgot why I had left my seat. I cancelled the trip to the restroom and went back to sit beside Frankie. Allison paused, her voice trailing off as the memories of that chaotic moment filled her thoughts.

Allison continued, in the beginning, Frankie used to take me everywhere until he lost his privilege with the cars. We owned a home together. Apparently, he didn't realise my parents were going bankrupt when dad lost his mental capacity to manage his financial affairs due to having Huntington's disease. Then, those that were running the businesses got corrupted when they learnt of dad's illness and mismanaged everything in order to profit from dad's predicament. Oh! How I wished I had stayed in law. My colleagues would have sorted them out.

In the meantime, unknown to me, Frankie was using most of our income in our joint account to fund his gambling habits. It's crazy, when you love and trust someone, you sometimes take things for granted and stop doing checks and balances. I didn't even know the extent of his gambling addictions then.

He used to visit casinos during those six-month intervals when he wasn't working and I was away at work.

I used to come home to a lovely home-cooked meal each evening, so I thought he was a good man, taking care of our home. Unknown to me, as soon as I left in the morning, he would hurry to cook and then be absent from the house all day, because he knew I worked long hours most of the time. He would even call to know when I would be home, then he would set the table and run the bath afterwards, making everything seem normal. I was completely oblivious.

Frankie could deceive anyone because he often appeared to be the picture-perfect family person. He would even fuss over ironing my work clothes. So, at one point when he suggested that we should let go of our helper, I thought he wanted us to save money. Little did I know that the money went straight to fund his addiction. He was a clever man indeed – very streetwise.

Then one day, everything unravelled. One day I came home from work and realised that we had lost our home. The bank changed the lock to our home. He was not even at home that day. He was out gambling. It was a hassle to even get our stuff from inside. When I queried the bank, confused because I paid the mortgage each month, they forwarded me the numerous correspondences and warnings. Turns out, all this time, Frankie had intercepted them.

Frankie actually cancelled the mortgage payments and used the money each month to gamble. I didn't think to check on that account because I had entrusted him with managing the household finances. When everything came to light, the shame was unbearable. To save face, I had to rent a house in another middle-class neighbourhood. At that time, I was now teaching and still working long hours. In the meantime, everything around me was falling apart - my dad's health was rapidly deteriorating, my parents' finances were in shambles and my health spiralling down too. I had a breakdown, but I kept it from my parents and Frankie, though I suspect he must have perceived it.

Meanwhile, Frankie was having fun. His neck was filled with chains probably weighing a kilogram each. He had tattoos everywhere including both sides of his head. He also sports a bull ring in his nose. He just kept adding different features to his body as if he wasn't comfortable in his own skin. Maybe he relished the attention he was attracting. But, he wasn't like that when we met. Not that anything was wrong with what he was doing, but it was the rapid change that unsettled me. I have never seen one person change so hastily. This version of Frankie was not the person I dated and agreed to marry. And then, as if all that wasn't enough, he went and had gold crowns on his front teeth to match his gold cargo necklaces. I thought he had overtaken the proverbial "Jones's" so to speak. People still adored him, though. He had this effortless charm that could win anyone over, but he had dual personalities. He often changed like the weather in England.

With no sports car to drive to have his usual get-a-ways, as our family business had been relocated offshore, Frankie was home more regularly in the evenings. Consequently, our home became almost like a war zone, more like a boxing arena to put it mildly. At times he would punch the walls with his fists when he couldn't get his own way. At other times, I became the wall. I was too scared and embarrassed to tell anyone. Although I was very close to my mum, I dared not tell her. That too had impacted my health. Support was readily available at work but I wanted to clearly separate my work life from family life, so I suffered in silence.

Frankie's parents were both accountants working for different firms. His dad, Marco, also had his own private accounting business that he operated from a converted garage at his home. Frankie was the youngest of his siblings and he rarely visited his parents due to sibling rivalry. They accused him of always wanting money, but his family was very shrewd and thrifty and so wasn't easily swayed. He couldn't play them like he did to my parents and me. When his dad put on his glasses and tilted it at the tip of his nose to address him, he had better change his mind if he was going to ask for money. They raised him well, but maybe they had been extremely strict, so he had built up an inner resentment. He couldn't take out his frustration on them directly, so as always, when that happens, you take it out on the closest person to you and in this case, I am sure you know who that was. At this point, Allison's voice faltered slightly, but she quickly straightened, unwilling to dwell on the obvious.

She continued, "His dad would "kill" him if I told the family what was going on. I dared not as I wouldn't want him to turn me into a pizza dough the moment we are back at home. I should have known better, Elsie, but it seemed that I was oblivious to the fact that I was living in abuse. I was expressing love that was not reciprocated. I guess love is blind to a lot of things even when one is being abused. It was really after our separation that I realised that, what I was putting up with, was actually domestic abuse. Often, he would start an argument followed by fights and verbal abuse. Then, like an eraser, he would wipe the pages all clean again acting all charming, lovely and romantic. This went on and on for a very long time.

It was only a few years later that I started to wonder if perhaps he was bipolar or had some other mental health issues? Or, was he just a thoughtless and uncaring person who knows how to play games to get what he wanted? I wished I had thought deep enough about these issues earlier. Maybe, I would have found a way to get him diagnosed and probably have a better understanding of what was happening to him, maybe this would have made a difference in our relationship. Who knows? Allison asked as she looked up at Elsie, a faint shrug in her shoulders, as if to say the answer was beyond her grasp.

> *Life is a teacher, and sometimes we need*
> *a bit of a lesson in hardship in order to learn.*
> *The question is, "Have I learnt?"*

8

ONE MAN'S MISSION
TO HELP OTHERS

Elsie (two days later, in an upbeat tone on the phone): "Top of the morning to you Dr Carey! How have you been, Sir? I had a very long and hectic two days, so I was unable to return your call. Sorry about that, sir."

Dr Carey: "Good morning, Elsie. I am so pleased to hear from you. Oh no! You don't have to apologise. I do understand. I called a bit late because I knew you were desperate to find someone to employ, and I didn't want you to miss the opportunity."

"Are you still looking for a carer for Mrs. Tamer Dunes, your mother-in-law?

Elsie (excited.) "Yes, Sir! Have you found someone?"

Dr Carey: "I have an interesting list of people from the agency, and a few of them stand out in particular."

Elsie: "Great! I know you will sort us out. You won't settle until you know your candidates and clients are well taken care of. It is therefore no surprise that you called my house so late from your office."

Dr Carey: "I looked at their applications, interviewed them, and three of them stood out in my mind. I somehow get the feeling that they are genuinely caring. They have been victims of circumstances in the past, and they are now seeking stability. Therefore, a full-time, live-in care opportunity would be ideal in order to give them a sense of belonging. At the same time, it would help to restore their dignity."

Dr: Carey (continued): "Elsie, you see, they are like prodigals, wanting to return home to normal life again. That must be part of the reason they came to our organisation. We are the voice and arms of the loving Father who seeks to embrace and restore His children. We do this through our services. As soon as anyone steps through our doors, the welcome home party begins, because we know that we are going to do everything possible to get them sorted."

"Listening to one in particular, a former lawyer and teacher, she reminded me of the frailty of humanity, and the fact that none of us is infallible regardless of status and prestige. She reminded me of this story as illustrated in the Great Guide Book:

> *"A man had two sons. The younger son told his father, 'I want my share of your estate now before you die.' So, his father agreed to divide his wealth between his sons.*
>
> *"A few days later this younger son packed all his belongings and moved to a distant land, and there he wasted all his money in wild living. About the time his money ran out, a great famine swept over the land, and he began to starve. He persuaded a local farmer to hire him, and the man sent him into his fields to feed the pigs. The young man became so hungry that even the pods he was feeding the pigs looked good to him. But no one gave him anything.*

"When he finally came to his senses, he said to himself, 'At home even the hired servants have food enough to spare, and here I am dying of hunger! I will go home to my father and say, "Father, I have sinned against both heaven and you, and I am no longer worthy of being called your son. Please take me on as a hired servant."

"So, he returned home to his father. And while he was still a long way off, his father saw him coming. Filled with love and compassion, he ran to his son, embraced him, and kissed him. His son said to him, 'Father, I have sinned against both heaven and you, and I am no longer worthy of being called your son.

"But his father said to the servants, 'Quick! Bring the finest robe in the house and put it on him. Get a ring for his finger and sandals for his feet. And kill the calf we have been fattening. We must celebrate with a feast, for this son of mine was dead and has now returned to life. He was lost, but now he is found.' So, the party began." (Luke 15:11-24 NLT)"

Elsie: "Wow! Doc. I can't wait to hear the story of that particular one- the former lawyer and teacher. Would she really take a live-in care job? She might be too expensive for us."

Elsie (continued): "Before I forget, Dr Carey, since the candidates just signed up to your agency only a few days ago, have you managed to get their police records processed yet?"

Dr Carey: "I am glad that you asked, because it is good to know that my clients feel reassured. We are a registered charity linked to the local government authority; therefore, safeguarding issues are essential. There is no compromise regarding that. None of our candidates are allowed to work with individuals until they are correctly processed, for the protection of themselves and those who will be caring for, like Mrs. Tamer Dunes, your mother-in-law."

Elsie: "Can I come to see you immediately, Dr Carey, to discuss further? I think our need for a carer has suddenly become more urgent than anticipated."

Dr Carey: "Yes, of course! I will be in the office almost all day, except I will have to leave at about 3pm for another engagement. However, even if you run late and miss me, the office will still be open. The secretary and counsellors will be there."

Elsie: "Can I make an appointment for 10:00am to discuss."

Dr Carey: "You are most welcome."

At the office, Dr Carey and Elsie ran through the list, and to Elsie's surprise, Allison Blackwell-Palmer was on it. She might be the prodigal he was referring to. Elsie believed that she might have wasted her parents' fortune. The notes taken at the interview stated that she would be underemployed as a carer due to her credentials. However, it also noted that she was likely to be an asset to any family as she was very good-tempered, able to provide mental stimulation and had great empathy. It further noted that she would prefer a job with the opportunity to live-in due to her circumstances.

The team at Charity Odyssey did ask Allison whether she had any other personal circumstances that might likely interfere with her performance on the job. Allison told how her dad passed away while in care from Huntington's disease. He used to be at home with two nurses employed to care for him but, when they lost the family home, he was taken into care. Her mum was currently staying indefinitely with a family friend.

Spikey, who interviewed her, immediately connected with her story. She confirmed that she recalled reading in the local newspaper the story of the Blackwell's family and how they lost everything in the recession. Their airline business went bankrupt as the stock market plummeted. Then, their automobile business moved offshore for operational efficiency. That was the last time her mother heard anything of that business.

Ever since, the case is still ongoing in court and the company that managed the automobile business has changed its name twice already. The director embezzled much of the money and left the company bankrupt. Apparently, he underhandedly sold it off to a third-party company. It is now operating under a different name. At the time, her father was too ill to even remember that they had businesses. Her mum had socially distanced herself since then due to the embarrassment of losing their home and businesses. It seemed, everyone in her neighbourhood was talking about it including former colleagues and friends. She also refused to attend the court hearings to defend the businesses. Even to accept empathy and assistance from significant others within her social circle became a problem due to embarrassment of perceived Chinese whispers.

Chinese whispers also had it that her mother's subtle resistance to the benevolent attitude of her close friends was due to pride and unending grief. Coupled with grieving the loss of her parents' fortune, Allison also had suffered a breakdown from her abusive husband of over 10 years. Upon discovering that information, I thought, "Wow! Should this be recorded? Should I also have access to all these details?" Then I looked again and the newspaper article had most of it.

Elsie's thoughts were immediately interrupted by Dr Carey. Dr Carey: "Elsie, you must be thinking how we managed to capture all this information in our interviews. We never pressure our candidates into giving information. We follow the Code of Conduct and the Care Value Base. We are also guided by different legislations including the Data Protection Act and Safeguarding of Vulnerable Adults Act. We only let clients see our candidates' records on a need-to-know basis and that includes you. Our candidates share freely due to the professional skills of our counsellors. Remember, we are a non-profit organization with the sole aim of helping employers to get our candidates back to operational efficiency. We do this through links and support from the government as well as private funding from local organisations and individuals. Therefore, the more information we can obtain from them, the more targeted our support can be. Moreover, while they are vulnerable, they are also consenting adults who can choose to select the information they give, except for those required for disclosure purposes."

Elsie: "Dr Carey, you are a mind reader. I was just about to ask and you satisfied my curiosity."

Dr Carey: "You see Elsie, our interviews are not viewed in a competitive sense like other profit-based companies who want to hire the most qualified and competent to maximise output and profit. Everyone that comes to us is viewed as qualified and competent. No matter their qualification and experience, our sole intent is to get them sorted. We also offer training if needed."

Our aim is to help sort them holistically and as best as we can. More importantly, if we can effectively counsel and get them into the right employment, then we would be helping to restore their dignity, self-esteem and sense of purpose. This would add meaning to their lives. With us, there is no win and lose situation. As long as they come through our doors, everyone's a winner, because they will be eventually sorted.

Look at our mission statement hanging on the wall over your head. It has its foundation embedded in Christ. It says,

> *"Come to me, all of you who are weary and carry heavy burdens, and I will give you rest." (Matthew 11:28 NLT).*

You see, we want to give them rest from their miseries and sufferings and restore hope. And it doesn't stop there. When we provide help, we also introduce them to Christ because,

> *"He heals the broken-hearted and binds up their wounds. (Psalm 147:3 NKJV.)*

We also show them in scripture what the sovereign Lord said,

> *"For I know the plans I have for you," says*
> *the LORD. "They are plans for good and not for*

disaster, to give you a future and a hope. (Jeremiah 29:11 NLT).

They all know that; this is a Centre of Hope.

Dr Carey: "Elsie, we also believe as an agency, that with the right support in place, we can instil hope, provide healing for people's minds and emotions combined with practical help. This includes: employment; opportunities to improve their skills set; training and shelter. With this in place, the galaxies will be the limit for these individuals. It will enable them to become the people they were designed to be."

Elsie nodded her head, thinking that Dr Carey wouldn't believe her if she told him that she knew Allison Blackwell-Palmer. Elsie wondered why Allison didn't remove Palmer from her surname. It seemed that was what had caused the extra baggage and trouble in her life. That Ex of hers – Frankie Palmer whom they coincidentally met, and was throwing tantrums like a toddler during the road incident. He had almost run Allison over on the road with his white van. He had treated her so inhumanely that day. However, the last time Elsie saw him, he seemed to be reinventing himself.

Dr Carey: "Elsie, as we listened to Allison speaking with such desperation, we sensed she wanted empathy and to be placed on our priority list for the next available position we have. However, what she didn't know is that everyone who comes to us is a priority case on our list. We desperately try to help them to get sorted, so that they can live a better life."

We also knew that Allison's steps had been ordered because there are many employment agencies in this locality. Some of them are even adjacent to us. They even offer part of their services for free, but she chose to walk through our doors. She came to us at Charity Odyssey, so we owe it to ourselves and to her, to get her sorted.

> *"The steps of a good man are ordered by the LORD, and He delights in his way" (Psalm 37:23 NKJV).*

Dr Carey (Continued): "Allison volunteered her information so freely and it is not uncommon based on the nature of our operational activities. Additionally, the people who conducted our interviews are all trained counsellors volunteering their time and they are always ready to offer support. Many of them started out with us in situations similar to Allison's. And, they have returned to give back some of the help that they once received. That is one of the reasons they are able to connect with our candidates so well, because they also share their own stories as a means of encouragement."

We also believe everyone's story is genuine until proven otherwise, either through police checks or their own admission prompted by a change of heart. However, even when the latter happens, we still offer support, hope and practical assistance. This is because we know that desperate people often do desperate things to survive. Therefore, no situation is ever too bad that it exceeds our ability to help; even if we have to outsource the help. We are non-judgemental in our approach. Hence, we use this abiding principle in conducting our affairs and that's why we consider our organisation to be effective and successful.

We often get testimonials from people across different racial profiling, languages and ethnicities commending our services. For example, Ben wrote to us last week after we helped him secure a job and reunite with his wife and children. When he first came to us, he was a heroin addict struggling to break free. He used to gamble everything away, and caused his family much pain and distress, including the loss of their family home. At one point, his children were taken into care. Today, Ben is now a wealthy financial broker and he too promised to volunteer with us soon. He kept thanking us for helping him to restore his life, family and dignity. He said our organisation reminded him of this verse:

> *"For there is hope for a tree,*
> *If it is cut down, that it will sprout again,*
> *And that its tender shoots will not cease.*
> *Though its root may grow old in the earth,*
> *And its stump may die in the ground,*
> *Yet at the scent of water it will bud*
> *And bring forth branches like a plant." (Job 14:7-9*
> *NLT).*

Had we not given Ben hope and watered his life with our resources, we might not have heard his testimony or from him ever again. Maybe we wouldn't even get the opportunity to help him change his life.

Our volunteers know the power of kindness and what it means to meet someone's needs at their lowest point. Like the incident of the mindless sheep in Eastern Turkey, many of them had once fallen over the cliff of life. But they were cushioned by the support they received, much like a soft, protective pile of wool, allowing them to recover and bounce back. Therefore, we believe in the golden rule:

"Do to others whatever you would like them to do to you." (Matthew 7:12 NLT).

This is one of the essences of life. As a result, we endeavour to continue to invest into people's lives, expecting to see returns in terms of more success stories and positive transformation of lives that will continue to inspire others, just like Ben's. We believe that helping others have a ripple effect, and it is no wonder our organisation keeps expanding.

"Give, and you will receive. Your gift will return to you in full—pressed down, shaken together to make room for more, running over, and poured into your lap. The amount you give will determine the amount you get back." (Luke 6:38 NLT).

Life is full of uncertainties. That's why helping others is important because no one knows how far the impact will reach. They or someone connected to them might need or be the one to offer similar help tomorrow. I learnt the following gem whilst growing up. It said:

"Never mock the stranger nor the poor. For you do not know what land you may travel, or what clothes you may wear before you die."

Therefore, I believe as the scripture said,

"Plant your seed in the morning and keep busy all afternoon, for you don't know if profit will come from one activity or another—or maybe both." (Ecclesiastes 11:6 NLT)

Elsie: "Dr Carey, you are incredible! How did you come up with the idea of setting up such an organisation? What inspired you? Was it the drive to self-actualise? You made me feel like I am listening to a sermon on the mount. Are you always like this, sociable and accessible? I had better focus on the files to see who I think might be right for us to hire."

Dr Carey: "Aw Elsie! You cannot be involved in this business if you are not personable. It would counter all effort. In helping, you have to be accessible to people in many ways. When I switched to private practice as a surgeon with the intent to make more money; I was immediately struck by the vast number of people who were still suffering, and couldn't access medical assistance due to affordability.

Some even died in the process of waiting for free treatment on the long waiting lists of many public hospitals. When I read about some of those cases in the local papers or saw them in the news, I was touched. I contacted one of the large, oversubscribed hospitals where I worked for many years and decided to open up my private practice to accommodate a few patients. The news spread quickly like the wildfires in California and Australia, and in no time, my practice became oversubscribed.

People were so desperate for medical assistance that, when they heard that our private practice was tending to a few patients for free, they were amazed. They came flooding into the surgery like they were going to the grocery store to stockpile for an impending natural disaster. At one point, our practice became overwhelming. Many of these people couldn't even afford their prescriptions, although the consultation and surgery fees were free. I had such empathy; I couldn't turn anyone away.

One afternoon, I sat in the surgery, reflecting on my childhood, specifically as a little boy with my grandmother waiting all day to see a doctor. Back then, I tackled a ball and fell, thinking I broke my ankle. The pain was so excruciating, my grandmother had to carry me most of the way. Another time, I recalled having mumps and thought my swollen face was going to explode. Those days my grandmother had not a penny, and we couldn't even afford bus fare. As a matter of fact, our village was so remote and underdeveloped that buses didn't run there. I remember we walked about six miles to get to the nearest hospital and she carried me most of the way.

Now, looking back, I thought, what if I had never been seen as a boy? I might not be here today as a man to administer care to other little boys like myself, waiting to be attended to, accompanied by their parents or grandparents. So, I decided to put aside my own personal interests and devote my time to helping others. I always believed, some way, somehow, things would work out in the end. I have not amassed a lot of wealth in tangible form, but the intangible benefits far outweigh the balance in my bank account. I wish those doctors who treated me yesterday, were around today for me to show my gratitude and to say to them,

> *"You have restored my health yesterday, so that I can now be in the same position today to do the same to others."*

I felt it was part of my moral obligations to help, so I did it for free. During my time at the surgery, we also ensured that every patient received the same standard of care. For instance, those patients who couldn't afford to pay, we treated them and offered an after-care service which lasted up to six months. We did this because we knew that health matters and health is wealth. Having good health is an asset, and a tangible investment for one's future. Each time I did a surgery for free, I kept hearing these words:

> *"For I was hungry and you gave me something to eat, I was thirsty and you gave me something to drink, I was a stranger and you invited me in, I needed clothes and you clothed me, I was sick and you looked after me, I was in prison and you came to visit me." (Matthew 25:35-36 NIV)*

At first, I thought, this was defeating the purpose for which I switched to private practice. I wanted to make more money, but instead, I was increasing my workload without being compensated financially. At the time, it never seemed to make much sense. However, the intrinsic rewards that restoring the infirm back to good health brings, in terms of seeing them doing things they couldn't do before, and the gratitude on their faces, is second to none.

In fact, it has been a blessing in disguise and an invaluable gift in knowing that I am doing it for those who cannot pay me back. I am also doubly encouraged by the scripture verse that says,

> *For God is not unjust. He will not forget how hard you have worked for him and how you have shown your love to him by caring for other believers, as you still do.' (Hebrews 6:10 NLT)*

Adding to that, each time I reflect, I am reminded of this verse because, at the time, I didn't know I was also planting seeds. It said:

It is no wonder, every one of our team members continue to enjoy good health to date, because we invested in the health of others. At times, we even risked our own health and family stability by working long hours amidst fatigue and sleep deprivation.

To our amazement, at the surgery, we never lacked anything. There was always provision at hand. We never ran out of surgical supplies, medicines or money. Often, the receptionist would call me and say, 'someone is on the phone to speak to you.' Many times, it was some organisation donating medical supplies or a philanthropist pledging to help finance us for a whole year and we didn't even know them. Even the government helped us because we helped to ease the burden on their services in local communities.

Years later, I started to consider the holistic needs of the community. I realised that there were people who didn't need to come to our surgery for medical attention but were living on the streets and in dire need. I don't like to see the homeless on the street corner, with that sort of grotesque look on their faces. Some scavenge the street for food while others set themselves alight, with chimneys of smoke coming out of their nostrils, giving off all kind of bizarre fragrances and behaviours. Still, others share needles and inject hard drugs into their bodies as if they were anesthesiologists preparing themselves and others for surgeries.

On my way home from surgery each day, I thought, there must be a way out for these people who are hopelessly trapped by the plight of their situations. They were like fishes in a big ocean of despair running into the nets of unsuspecting fishermen every day. I thought, I need to do something. I need to be a part of a rescue mission to help protect them and to give them hope and a better way of life. This would include meeting their basic needs, such as: food, clothing, shelter, counselling and gainful employment.

I also believed that some of these people had latent talent ready to be tapped into. I wanted to help them release their creativity by coming up with their own business ideas and solutions. Then provide a means for them to market it. Each evening, I would see a group of people who had lost their way and their dignity, and needed to be restored as a matter of urgency. Then I thought of the scripture verse,

> *"For he will rescue you from every trap and protect you from deadly disease. He will cover you with his feathers. He will shelter you with his wings."* (Psalm 91:3-4 NLT)

I reflected and concluded that there must be a way in which I could play a role in fulfilling this scripture verse to rescue these hopeless people.

Then I said to myself, that's what I need to do for them. I need to see that verse fulfilled in their lives. Therefore, if I could find a way to give these people a new life, then I would be rescuing countless others from falling into the same trap. For instance, if only I could help rescue the heroin addict from contracting deadly diseases by providing rehabilitation to change their lifestyles and routines, then they could be meaningfully engaged in training and employment.

If only I could help sort shelter for all who recognize that they need it and are willing to accept the offer. As you wouldn't believe that some homeless people do not always accept the help given to them. I have known of acquaintances who have taken homeless people off the streets without even knowing them and put them into their own private homes. Nevertheless, within a couple of days, they gave excuses, saying that the family was too nice and they didn't want to be a burden, so they returned to the streets. If only I could find a way to help them rise mentally, to visualise themselves out of their predicament. Then, they would be able to arise from their fallen state, and it would be much easier to help them.

So, I decided that I needed to do something tangible for this sect of people when I retired. I thought that I needed to be a light, even a candle in this dark world, so that others could find their way back on the right path to wholeness again. I wanted to provide a place of refuge, a sanctuary away from the various traps set by the fowlers of life. These include the trap of alcoholism, drug abuse, homelessness, distress, hunger, unemployment, abuse, hopelessness, etc. Then I thought, "I might not be able to solve every problem, but I should be able to make a difference."

"Elsie," said Dr Carey, "You see, life has no meaning if you are not trying to lift someone out of the abyss that they found themselves in. It could be as simple as giving someone a meal to rid them of the pain of hunger at that moment, thereby lifting their spirits. But whatever little you can start with, would be a start in the right direction."

I believe someone has lifted each of us in some way or form, so we should in return, try to lift others. We should not push them further into the abyss of hopelessness and despair, with our arrogant and callous attitude of negligence. People matter and we all matter to God. Until we start to think that way, the helpless will continue to receive no help. The hopeless will continue to receive no hope, and the hungry will go on starving.

One evening, I stopped and tried to speak to a seemingly lost soul on the street, and he made me cry. Did you know that some people want to get out of the traps of life, but they can't find their way? Will you help?

> *Remember, the good that you do today,*
> *are seeds sown for tomorrow.*

9

A HOLIDAY GONE MAD

Frankie wanted children and they were taking too long to arrive. He never got checked to see whether he had anything to do with the delay. However, he blamed it all on me. He said that he wanted boys so that he could play football with them at home and teach them how to wrestle. Since they weren't there, he wrestled with me instead.

Allison continued: "Listen to this, Elsie. Frankie got me so upset one morning."

I said to him, "Frankie, breakfast is ready."

Frankie (Came into the kitchen diner immediately. The table was well laid): "What's the occasion?" He asked.

Allison: "Have you forgotten that it is our first wedding anniversary, sweetheart?"

Without saying a word, Frankie hissed through his teeth and walked away from the breakfast table.

Allison: "So uncouth," I thought.

Elsie: "Oh wow! Uncouth indeed."

Allison: "Yes, I thought he was so uncouth and unappreciative but I remained calm."

Frankie (Came back to the breakfast table): "Is that all? Why didn't you book a pub breakfast instead?" He chuckled then went upstairs.

A few minutes later, he returned again to the breakfast table to eat. Maybe he was on some form of substance.

Allison (continued with tears flooding her hazel eyes): "Elsie, I deserved it! I should have listened to my parents' advice. I should have listened to my gut feelings, and I should have also listened to my Vicar. I needed a whole lesson on listening and following instructions in my own life. I should have known better than to feed him too. A well laid table and he didn't contribute to financing it or help with any of the preparations either. As the scripture says, *"... if a man does not work, he should not eat."* *(2 Thessalonians 3:10 NLV)*

Allison: "Elsie, during our meal, I got up to add some scrambled eggs, beans and hash browns to the bacon on the table. Within a few minutes, I heard the chinaware rattle, then smash on to the white ceramic tiled floor. You would have thought it was the result of an earthquake tremor. The sound was alarming. Splinters, food and liquid were everywhere. The white tablecloth resembled bandages from a gunshot wound.

Elsie (speechless): "What! Did the table legs give way?"

Allison: "No!" I looked around but Frankie was absent. The table was still intact. I thought the earth had sucked him in. I was not amused. I was in distress. "Where are you?" I enquired. "What happened?"

I was just asking questions but no one was there to answer.

Frankie (Amused, returning with a mop, broom and pan in his hand whilst grinning): "Just chill!" "My phone fell and I reached over to grab it and the table cloth got stuck into my watch band and then everything slid off the table."

Allison: "I looked at him in amazement as he handed me the mop and broom for me to do the cleaning. I often wondered whether he did it on purpose. Then I remembered a chat I had with a friend prior to dating him. She had just ended a relationship. She told me not to waste good things on people who will not appreciate them. She also added that some people didn't even deserve it either. I later discovered the verse in the bible that she was referring to:

> *"...Don't throw your pearls to pigs! They will trample the pearls, then turn and attack you. (Matthew 7:6 NLT).*

"Believe me Elsie, it is sad to say, but I have proven this to be so true. Maybe I shouldn't say it, and I beg your pardon, but Frankie is a PIG! Yes, a muddy, smelly one too. His attitude stunk most of the time, similar to a pig's pen that has been left unattended. He was also a large guy, so a cow maybe would also be an equally fitting description. Still, I forgave him, just for the preservation of our marriage and out of love. No! Maybe it was out of stupidity."

Not long after that incident, we managed to take a holiday. We went on a Caribbean cruise and did some island hopping. We decided to spend a few days in St. Lucia and then catch up with the ship later as some people often do. It was all planned. We didn't have relatives there. In St. Lucia, he attacked me in the national reserve park over a simple joke about a past event that had nothing to do with us. He punched me in the face and spat at me. I began to cry but soon mopped it up and walked back to our hotel. Later, I asked him, 'Frankie, are you ok?' This time the thought definitely crossed my mind that he might be suffering from bi-polar disorder. That night in our hotel suite, we had live wrestling and you know who obviously won.

Yet I forgave him again. The next day, we boarded the tour bus and stopped at the fruit vendors along the way up the hill. We bought mangoes, coconut jelly, sugar cane and many other fruits. Being adventurous, halfway through the tour, we abandoned the bus and went on a picnic instead.

Whilst sitting on a wooden bench in the park, eating some of the fruits, down came a shower of rain like bullets on our heads. It was still sunny, so we wondered where it came from. We were unprepared and therefore our clothes were soaked. One could see the print of our coloured underwear. He then got angry, blamed me and asked why we didn't stay on the tour bus. He started to curse then slapped me across the face when I answered back. As if that was not enough, he broke off a branch and started hitting me with it. Maybe I reminded him of the children he so desperately wanted to have.

Then the rain suddenly stopped. The sun began beating down again and I just ran away not knowing where I was going. As I ran, I could feel my clothes drying in the heat and cool breeze. He searched frantically for me but I hid in one of several caves in the woods. He went away and came back about 45 minutes later. I was still hiding and shivering. I thought, what if scorpions and other insects were in the cave. I prayed. A million thoughts came flooding through my mind.

Being constantly on the lookout, I peeped and saw four men; three in uniform, searching frantically and yelling, "Allison! Allison! Allie! Alice! Allie!" His voice was distinct from the others. I kept quiet and asked the Lord for help as I saw them pop in and out of other caves and were coming towards mine. I was terrified. My heart sank. Goose pimples spread all over me. I started choking with fear. I thought, were they looking to genuinely save me or, did they want to get rid of me in the woods so that he could be free of me forever? Negative thoughts raced through my mind and every fibre of my being because I was still very angry with him. Will it be a happy ending? Since I couldn't answer any of those rhetorical questions, I tried to keep calm and quiet but still on the alert.

Allison: "Elsie, I even wondered why I came on holiday with him knowing how terrible he can be. Day by day, my love and trust for him began to erode.

'What would happen to me if they ever found me?' I thought."

Then, suddenly, they stood in front of my cave. I was petrified. I froze. It was as if my mind drew them to it. "O Lord, Help!" I thought to myself. Then like a movie screen flashing in front of me again, I remembered my parents and how happy I was when he came to our house asking them for my hand in marriage. I quickly turned the memory off and realised that I was still holding my miniature blue Gideons pocket bible that I take everywhere with me. This time I couldn't read it physically as it was still soaked and the pages clung to each other. I was also shaking from fright, and the sunset was throwing shadows over the already poorly lit cave.

I instead tried to remember some scripture verses, but it seemed like my memory froze too. Then suddenly I recalled: *"What I always feared has happened to me. What I dreaded has come true." (Job3:25 NLT)* I was so nervous; my pocket bible fell from my hand. I thought they must have heard the sound. I thought, this is it, I am going to die now.

I saw everyone looking and contemplating whether to enter my cave. I heard one of the officers said, "That could be the sound of insects or lizards jumping around or it could be our imagination." Then another said, "It's getting late and we don't have time to waste. Look! No-one is in that cave!"

"How do you know?" Another asked. Then the other officer replied, "Don't you see that cobwebs have covered the entrance to the cave?" "If someone went in, it would have been broken." That explanation seemed to have satisfied them and with that, they disappeared from view.

As I listened, I knew it was the result of Divine intervention. "I knew it! I knew it! "I thought. "I knew God would show up to help me. Otherwise, how else could that have happened to a cave that I went into less than two hours earlier?" Then I heard in my mind:

> *"He will cover you with his feathers. He will shelter you with his wings. His faithful promises are your armor and protection." (Psalm 91:4 NLT).*

Allison: "Elsie, when I was much younger, my parents usually tell me that studying and memorizing the scriptures was never a waste of time. That it was mankind's greatest weapon for those who have discovered and know how to use it. They said, the beauty of it was, if I were ever to be in trouble, I could always extract that weapon anytime from within. That day, their words came to pass. They must have been following these instructions themselves each time they teach me the scriptures:

> *"So, commit yourselves wholeheartedly to these words of mine. Tie them to your hands and wear them on your forehead as reminders. Teach them to your children. Talk about them when you are at home and when you are on the road, when you are going to bed and when you are getting up. Write them on the doorposts of your house and on your gates, so that as long as the sky remains above the earth, you and your children may flourish in the land the LORD swore to give your ancestors. "Be careful to obey all these commands I am giving you. Show love to the LORD your God by walking in his ways and holding tightly to him." (Deuteronomy 11:18-22 NLT)*

About two hours later as the sun was setting, I left the cave. It was like a maze finding my way back to the hotel. I wanted to report the domestic abuse, but I was unsure of the laws of the island and how Frankie would have reacted. I prayed instead to get back home safely to see my mother – a long way home to another continent.

When we finally arrived home from our holiday on the cruise, there was another surprise awaiting us. This time, our belongings were out in the garden whilst some were at the entrance to the gate. Everything was scattered as if some homeless person had already helped themselves to some of our possessions. Frankie got angry and called the landlord. He came promptly and asked if we didn't receive the eviction notice. I was shocked. Then he said he had been owed seven months' rent. I couldn't believe it. I attacked Frankie right in front of the landlord. I told him that because of his addiction, we lost our home, and now our rented accommodation. I was fuming on the inside.

Then I said to him in subtle anger, "You begged for forgiveness and vowed that you would be more responsible this time. I forgave you and I gave you the rental money each month to pay." "What have you done with it?" He stared at me as if I wasn't making sense to him.

Frankie had gambled it all away again. I should have known better than to give him access to our finances again. But he kept insisting that he was the head of the house by design and that he was reformed. I allowed his controlling and manipulative attitude to keep dominating our decisions, even though I knew better. Nonetheless, for the sake of peace, I kept giving in.

The next day, I went to the bank to check on my other account, and it too was empty. Adding to that pain, I then came to realise that whilst we were on holiday, my mum lost the family home. No wonder I received so many missed calls from her, but we had signal issues at sea. Mum had to move in with a family friend which is another story. It then became too much. I was still recovering from the loss of my dad, the loss of both our homes, and now; the loss of my childhood home which had left mum homeless. Losses seemed to have become normative within my family, and everything was now taking its toll on us.

Can you imagine? The same night we returned from holiday, I had to sleep on the street because mum too had lost her home. It was sudden. There was nowhere to go and no money to shelter in a hotel room. The homeless shelters were also full. It sounded pretty much like the birth of Jesus when his parents couldn't find any room in the Inn.

Frankie didn't even stay with me that night. He just went his way. He also didn't argue, though I was trying to make a fuss of it all. That showed how callous he had become. Maybe he knew what was awaiting us upon returning. Maybe he had worked out a contingency plan ahead of time for himself. He must have had one, but it obviously didn't include me. Maybe he was glad when I tried to make a fuss with him so he could use it as an alibi to leave me on my own that night. Ever since we have been separated, I had only seen him a few times in many years. The last time was when we left the café and he tried to run me over with his white van.

It's not good to keep 'beating up' oneself over past events, but I should have listened! I wished I had! One day mom and dad sat me down and said, "Allie our little darling, listen to us. We know how it feels when you are young and starting to fall in love. However, if you are thinking about dating or marrying someone who doesn't share a similar belief system and moral values as you, don't do it!" "You can easily be led astray, and it will hinder your relationship with Christ. Don't think that he will change when you get married. That is quite rare, and it will most likely cause more problems and regrets."

"Did I listen to them? No! My dad would often say, "You might forget our words, but you will never forget the Word of God. Even if you don't follow them now, they will flash back in your mind to haunt you later." Then he would turn the pages of his large print parallel study bible and read verses from two different versions to enable me to understand clearly. This version stood out vividly in my mind ever since:

> *"Don't become partners with those who reject God. How can you make a partnership out of right and wrong? That's not partnership; that's war. Is light best friends with dark? Does Christ go strolling with the Devil? Do trust and mistrust hold hands?" (2 Corinthians 6:14 -15 MSG).*

A couple of years after our wedding, one night whilst Frankie was out, I rolled over in bed, and that scripture verse surfaced like a still picture. Then, it was as if my mattress was filled with needles due to a manufacturing fault during production. I couldn't sleep. I rolled and tossed trying to find a comfortable spot, but to no avail. I moved to another room but every bed felt the same, so I moved back to our room. I cried and cried because it seemed I couldn't escape the haunting thoughts. I then reflected on how different my life would have been had I heeded God's words and my parent's instructions.

Frankie and I turned out to be like oil and water. No matter how you shake the two together, they still separate. Only divine intervention could make our relationship work. Also, a friend had cautioned me, "Never say never. Tomorrow, who knows, he might just become a new creature in Christ." I doubted that very much but she continued by quoting this verse:

"This means that anyone who belongs to Christ has become a new person. The old life is gone; a new life has begun!" (2 Corinthians 5:17 NLT)

Whether my parents were discerning or had their intuition from experience, it was as if they knew. Initially, I didn't disclose much about Frankie to them, worried that they might disapprove of our relationship. In hindsight, I realised I didn't know much about him either. However, from the onset, I was unsure whether he was God-fearing because he seldom ever entertains anything on the subject. However, I thought he was a secret disciple.

When Frankie was in my parents' presence, he always tried to put his best foot forward. However, my parents always tell me that each time he leaves the house, there was something about him that made them uneasy. But they couldn't really pinpoint what it was. They said they never felt at peace when he was around. Consequently, they cautioned me to be careful. They actually wanted to investigate further, but I prevented them. I thought their regular counselling was a bit old fashioned and maybe, even a bit prejudiced. Now I realise that I was so wrong. Now, my advice to anyone is: b*efore investing, investigate.* It doesn't matter whether it's a relationship, a business venture or buying a home.

However, it still seemed bizarre how we came together. I was in the church choir, focused and fun loving with not a care in the world, except for work. I was really enjoying life. Then I met Frankie. He was a charmer and seemed very honest about his past and how he had been rehabilitated. As a reformed smoker, drinker and gangster, he had turned his life around and graduated from university two years before me. He also had a problem with his temper. As a result, he once did community services for minor assault. Later, he became gainfully employed and used to work long hours.

At the time, he seemed so sincere and eager to have the family that he always dreamt about. Whenever we met, whether on a date or just randomly ran into each other on the street, I knew it was going to be a wonderful moment. He was very personable, affectionate, full of charisma, polite and creative in making one smile even on the greyest days. He could turn any gloomy situation into laughter and he never worried about anything. A very positive person indeed, I thought. His plans for a family seemed so perfect, and I thought everyone deserves a second chance, hence, why not Frankie. Again, maybe I was wrong.

From this experience, I have learnt that it never pays to compromise on values and principles. When I slowly began to unfold to my mum what was happening, immediately she quoted this verse to me and I was amazed. She said:

> *"But I am not surprised! Even Satan disguises himself as an angel of light." (2 Corinthians 11:14 NLT).*

*He*r words pierced my heart like a dagger and I bled internally without her knowing it. I turned to my dad, as we were also very close, and he was very protective of me. He too was irate about Frankie's behaviour, but knowing my parents, their only weapon for every situation was the Word of God. He put the devotional he was reading on the side table beside the sofa. Then he took up the little pink and green floral inspirational book filled with thoughts of wisdom and encouragement that they both gave to me on my sixteenth birthday. Then he said, "This was a very important item that you left behind at home when you got married. I always thought its content would still be relevant, whatever stage of life you were at." He then read from page 13:

> *"Beware of false prophets who come disguised as harmless sheep but are really vicious wolves. You can identify them by their fruit, that is, by the way they act. Can you pick grapes from thorn bushes, or figs from thistles? A good tree produces good fruit, and a bad tree produces bad fruit. A good tree can't produce bad fruit, and a bad tree can't produce good fruit."* (Matthew 7:15-18 NLT.)

After dad read it to me, I hugged him and confessed. I said, "Dad, I didn't know Frankie for that many years I told you and mom. I lied to you both. I must admit. I did it because he was so charming and I didn't want to lose him. I wanted both of your approval." Upon hearing that, dad shook his head and cried. He then hugged me and said he forgave me. He also reminded me how they used to tell me, each time Frankie visited, that they had an uneasy feeling about him. However, I was not willing to listen, he said. I knew what he was saying was very true. Frankie and I speed-dated our relationship. So, I never waited long enough to see what fruits he was bearing.

Obviously, Frankie never got delivered from his demons. He was able to camouflage himself in order to impress me because he realised that I was naïve. I was naïve because he was my first date. He turned out to be a vicious wolf in sheep's clothing combined with the charming tongue of a serpent. I was surprised when dad said he knew. He said he didn't want us to keep arguing since I was so strong-headed in defending Frankie. Then dad added that I also behaved as if I knew it all, just because I had just graduated from law school. He said he knew it was only a matter of time before I would come running back to them. Also, sometimes, the best way forward for someone who doesn't listen, is for them to learn through experience.

Allison continued: "Obviously, as you can see Elsie, I have learnt the hard way. Dad was correct. I can tell you now, experience is a real teacher. Dad also said that he and mum thought I would use the same strong-headedness to get out of any situation that I found myself in. As a result, they never really worried about me. This time though, they got it wrong. I was strong-headed in defending Frankie, but I was not strong headed towards Frankie. This is because, early on into our marriage, he managed to break my spirit through intimidation and abuse. He left me so emotionally traumatized that my sense of self-worth had diminished.

Then my dad held my hands and said, "Allie darling, though damaging at times, sometimes the best teacher is experience. For instance, fire is attractive. If a child keeps poking his fingers at an open flame and you keep shielding him by telling him that it will hurt badly if he touches it. However, if the child kept throwing tantrums in wanting to touch it, what would you do? I am afraid, in such a situation, only a small encounter with the fire can become his real teacher. Even if the child didn't touch it in your presence, when the child sees it elsewhere, he might still want to touch it regardless. We knew you were associating with fire, but we couldn't get you to listen. We also knew that you would return some day to tell us or even show us the evidence of touching it. But we just didn't know how soon."

Allison: Dad continued, "To be honest darling, although it was at the back of our minds that it might happen, I still cannot believe what I am hearing from you. No parent wants that to happen to their child." He then hugged me and wept again.

I have never seen dad cry in all my life, but on that occasion, he did, several times. I was thankful for my parents' love and empathy, but at the same time, I was angry with myself for not following their advice.

I didn't have control over what Frankie was doing to me, I could only control myself. I made sure that I treated him well, even though it was not reciprocated.

Going forward, would I adjust how I treat a future spouse? Absolutely not! Except perhaps to treat him even better. I gave my best to Frankie and I would still give my best to any future spouse. I would not let how Frankie treated me restrain my love towards another person. The fact that he was unable to see, appreciate and receive my love, is his own loss. Sooner rather than later, he will wake up from his stupor.

I still believe that there is someone out there who is praying to God for a virtuous, loving and respectful wife like me, and I pray that divine providence will connect us. Let's hope it happens soon enough before Frankie wakes up and starts searching for me. People often don't recognise value until they lose it. Is love blind?

> *People often don't recognize value until they lose it.*

10

FINDING ENCOURAGEMENT

Whilst watching snowboarding on SKY TV during the Sochi 2014 Winter Olympics, in the heat of the excitement when some skaters were crashing and tumbling over, one commentator remarked, "If you are skating and an arm comes off, leave it behind and keep going". I have seen athletes do that time and time again in terms of continuing to compete in spite of their injuries.

In that same year, during the Commonwealth games held in Glasgow, whilst watching the semi-final of the men's 4x100m relay, something similar happened. As the gun went off, and the athletes dashed out of their starting blocks running towards the baton exchange; within 50 metres of the race, one of the Jamaican sprinters suffered a pulled muscle and began limping. Despite his injuries, he carried on and went as quickly as he could to pass the baton to his team mate. They carried on until the baton was passed to Usain Bolt, world's fastest athlete at the time who was running the anchor leg. Although he was in a disadvantaged position when he received the baton, Bolt bolted to the finish line and won. This enabled the Jamaican quartet not only to win the semi-final, but also to qualify for, and eventually win the final.

However, it all started with one man who defied negative emotions and physical pain from a pulled muscle to focus on the joy of his team winning. He used his head to decide what to do, and not what he was experiencing or feeling at that moment. Another SKY TV commentator noted, "Pulling up and lying on the track would have been the natural thing for the athlete to do." Yet another continued, "He even risked not participating in the up-coming world championships because, by continuing to run after being injured, he ran the risk of worsening it. He might even miss an entire season as a result, which could put his personal career on hold."

Elsie: "Allison, those athletes who had the gold medal in view and worked towards it, are the ones who trade their temporary comfort and even suffered in order to win. Winning is a process. It often involves pain, inconvenience, focus, commitment, consistency and hard work. Consequently, we must all have some goal in front of us to keep us inspired, and to do whatever it takes to bring them to fruition, amidst the setbacks and difficulties that life often throws at us."

In other words, each day, you should have a set target, a goal or a plan that you are practically working towards that will inspire you to keep going amidst the challenges of life.

However, often, this can only be accomplished with the help of God and heeding to what he tells you to do. We see Jesus, though he was God in the flesh, focused on his goal and destination in front of him. Hence, when the difficulties came, they couldn't distract him from his purpose. I like how this version of scripture puts it. It states,

> *"Keep your eyes on Jesus, who both began and finished this race we're in. Study how he did it. Because he never lost sight of where he was headed— that exhilarating finish in and with God—he could put up with anything along the way: Cross, shame,*

Therefore, whatever you do, never give up! Never quit! Pursue your goals amidst all the setbacks of life. Those abandoned projects, return to them and start pursuing them again. For instance, if you are studying, whether it is for a career change or just to improve your skills set and you are experiencing challenges in passing certain courses, stay focused. Study harder, attend tutorials, acquaint yourself with the right course materials and get a study partner. Always keep your eyes set on the qualification that you will receive at the end. The value or worth of that qualification is something that should keep you inspired. Picture yourself in your graduation gown. Picture hearing your name being called for the award. Picture walking confidently to the podium to receive your qualification, and you eventually will. That's what I did in a similar circumstance.

I remember when I was working full-time and doing post graduate studies. The professor who was assigned to oversee my dissertation told me that I couldn't complete it within the time frame I had set. He frankly stated that it was impossible balancing it with full time employment. As a result, he went on a long holiday and didn't offer me any support whatsoever. But I never gave up or gave in to his negative pronouncement. That was the extent to which he could see. I had a vision that extended far beyond. In the end, he said to me, "You said you could do it and you certainly did." Yes! I successfully completed my post graduate studies and graduated within that same time frame. Was it easy? Certainly not."

With Allison's beautiful hazel eyes glued to me, intently listening to what I was saying, I continued to encourage her not to let her past rob her of visualising and taking advantage of the great future which lay ahead. I encouraged her to use her imagination combined with action, rather than dwelling on her memories. This is because imagination inspires creativity. This then can take anyone out of stagnation and propel them to new heights. Conversely, memory often ties people to the past and this can kill their potential. Memory often keeps one looking in the rear-view mirror instead of looking ahead. This not only slows you down in life, but it could prove fatal to your destiny if you are not paying attention to what's happening ahead. As a result, a lot of people have missed great opportunities, including myself.

Don't get me wrong, some memories are good. Nevertheless, they are still past events, actions, activities or achievements which could become counterproductive and hinder future growth and development, if you dwell on them too long. Sometimes, yesterday's achievement can become tomorrow's hindrances as it makes one become complacent. The same can be applied to losses too. Let it go and move forward. Always remember, greater and better things are still ahead, so keep trying. Keep pushing the boundaries. Start again.

Ask yourself, what greater exploit can I accomplish today?

What am I doing today that will make my tomorrow better than yesterday?

When I was in primary school, I learnt this little memory gem which, although sounds simple, is full of inspiration. Our teacher usually made us recite it at the top of our lungs at the start of every lesson each day:

"Good, better, best. Never let it rest. Until, your good is better, and your better best."

It became our little anthem and even going to bed at nights, I could unconsciously hear myself saying it. It became so entrenched within that it wouldn't allow me to procrastinate with my homework or studies. So, in her class, if you were writing, and your essay didn't meet her standards, you would have to re-write it until you achieve the best. It is no wonder that one of my essays got published in one of the nation's top newspapers whilst at primary school, from a national competition our school had entered. It felt like our teacher was a perfectionist, and in essence, she was. But she also wanted us to maximize our potential. Looking back, most of us did. We didn't settle for the status quo. We always aimed at doing better and kept moving forward no matter the situation. It was a great value she had instilled in us.

Years later, it was that same little gem that reminded me that I had actually been stagnated. Although I had achieved some of life's "toy", I had stopped accomplishing. Instead, I was looking at, playing with and polishing the toys that I had acquired yesterday. They had become beautiful trophies and I was not doing anything to increase the collection.

I suddenly woke up and realised that I should have been trading those "toys" globally by now. Years had passed by and in the process, I missed out on a number of opportunities.

I never allowed my "good" to become "better" nor my "better" to become "best", so to speak. Since then, I have moved on and so should you."

Elsie: "Allison, with determination and drive, start imagining great things again. Think like little children who are very imaginative and keep seeing endless possibilities. Sometimes they just make things up and often, those same things become reality later on. These days, they even think far beyond the skies because they already know that becoming an astronaut and travelling to the moon is possible. They know that becoming a billionaire is possible, so they are thinking about things like being the first to explore other planets or being the first to perform a human head transplant. They keep pushing boundaries. As adults, that's what we should also do—keep scaling new heights.

> *Jesus said to him, "If you can believe, all things are possible to him who believes." (Mark 9:23 NKJV)*

That's how we were wired by our creator, to do great things – things that exceed human expectations. Another scripture verse puts it this way:

> *"Now all glory to God, who is able, through his mighty power at work within us, to accomplish infinitely more than we might ask or think." (Ephesians 3:20 NLT)*

With reference to children, the pictures they create in their minds are only tampered with when they begin to socialize. Sometimes adults, including their teachers and parents, would often correct them by telling them that what they are thinking about wasn't possible. When they do that, they are placing limits on their young minds as to what they could accomplish. It's like cutting down a potentially fruit bearing tree in an orchard, thinking that you have enough of the same kind. However, that one tree might just be different. It could be of the same species but bear a different shape, taste and colour of fruit. You might just be surprised.

Some adults see obstacles based on their own reality and experiences, but children often see possibilities because they have no past experience to contaminate their minds. So, when they erect empires in their heads, it is often reduced to rubble by some thoughtless or even good-willed individuals. However, those that grow up in environments that nurture their gifts, will eventually realise their potential.

It's like comparing faith and doubt. Doubt usually sees impossibilities whilst faith sees a world of possibilities. Doubt focuses on darkness whilst faith sees the path illuminated with light. Doubt fears to venture out but faith takes a leap of faith into the unknown, like the Apostle Peter who dared to walk on water. That wonder had never been done before. Peter's audacious move depicted great faith:

> *And Peter answered Him and said, "Lord, if it is You, command me to come to You on the water."*
>
> *So, He said, "Come." And when Peter had come down out of the boat, he walked on the water to go to Jesus. (Matthew 14: 28-29 NKJV)*

Apostle Peter was a grown adult, yet he had faith like a child. He believed anything was possible. If you study his life, you will see that he went on to do some amazing things, because he was acquainted with Jesus. It is no wonder scriptures recorded,

> *But Jesus looked at them and said to them, "With men this is impossible, but with God all things are possible." (Matthew 19:26 KJV)*

It is no surprise that we see these words of Jesus in the preceding chapter:

> *Then Jesus called a little child to Him, set him in the midst of them, and said, "Assuredly, I say to you, unless you are converted and become as little children, you will by no means enter the kingdom of heaven (Matthew 18:3 NKJV)*

So, don't stay in your comfort zone. Don't be idle. Like Apostle Peter, venture out to try something new or different. As scripture puts it:

> *The lazy man says, "There is a lion in the road!*
> *A fierce lion is in the streets!"*
> *As a door turns on its hinges,*
> *So does the lazy man on his bed.*
> *(Proverbs 26:13-14 NKJV)*

I know of people who would not even venture out to try a new cuisine in this multicultural society. They think that they are going to get food poisoning or the food won't be as good. They are stuck in their culture and belief system. They are not open-minded and it often limits their association, freedom, creativity and potential to experience novelty. They settle for "good" and ignore "better" and, even "best" when they come knocking.

I spent five years working in an organization. Later, I came across a better paying post within my same field and it came with a promotion. It was a much larger organization that had a higher profile. I was telling a few close colleagues at my organization that I was going to apply for the post because it comes with a promotion. One of my colleagues, Denny, gave me a stern warning not to venture out as I was already in a permanent post. In his exact words, he said, *"A known devil is better than an unknown one."* I thought about it and acknowledged that it could be true, but it never deterred me from applying and stepping out by faith from where I was.

I knew that new levels bring new challenges or new devils as he had warned. I also knew that it takes wisdom to manage challenges. Also, if managed in the right way, challenges can result in further growth and development. People are paid to manage challenges, after all, things are not always expected to be smooth sailing all the time. Nevertheless, I applied for the post and got it. Was it challenging? Certainly, but it was within my scope to manage. I spent seven years there then moved on to an even higher managerial post that I am still currently at.

I happened to return to my former workplace about 12 years later to attend an event. Surprisingly, I saw Denny, my former colleague and he was still in the same post at the same level. As a matter of fact, he was the only person remaining from our group. Everyone had moved on and have been climbing the career ladder, yet he was still asking me about the challenges we face stepping out. Then he began to make the same quote, *"A known devil is better than an unknown one."* I just looked at him and grinned.

Then I thought to myself, step out, even for your children's sake. Be a role model to them, challenging them to grow and achieve. Interestingly, Denny was not alone. His wife had also been in the same post at the same level in a similar organization for years. Nothing is wrong in remaining in an organization. Commitment is important, but at the same time, you should be growing. You should be stepping up the career ladder or whatever you are involved in. As a matter of fact, anything you are involved in, you should ensure that you experience growth and development. Even your relationship with God and people should experience new dimensions.

Interestingly, each time I reflect on that former colleague and his wife, all that comes to mind is the following scripture, and I like how this version puts it. It says,

> *Loafers say, "It's dangerous out there! Tigers are prowling the streets!" and then pull the covers back over their heads. (Proverbs 26:13 MSG).*

People like Denny, my former colleague, whilst they sleep, opportunities pass them by. They often don't know that many times, the tiger they fear is a figment of their imagination. Their minds are as timid as rabbits and it keeps them limited and from fulfilling their destinies. It's keeping them from pursuing and achieving greater things. Denny should have asked Apostle Peter, and he would tell him that stepping out of the boat and walking on water is not easy, but it brings fulfilment and a great feeling of accomplishment. It fuels your adrenaline and makes you feel invincible, wanting to raise the bar each time you venture into a new project. Also, like Apostle Peter, the Master whose call you have responded to, will be right there to help in case of any eventualities. When you step out of the boat of life, there is no limit to what you can accomplish.

"Allison, in life, you must dare to step out amidst the challenges you are currently facing. Dare to challenge yourself to improve. Dare to attempt great things even with limited resources. One person puts it this way, "If the dream is big enough, the facts don't count." You don't have to see it physically before you make a positive move towards it. Visualize and act. Dare to go against the status quo. Dare to acquire new skills sets. Dare to keep moving forward and upward despite the obstacles."

If you don't give up, you will win. Sometimes the boat might even be rocked as you try to step out. This is because many people do not want you to leave them behind in the boat. As a result, moving away might create discontent, but you must step out regardless. Dare to "rock the boat" if you must, but whatever you do, don't stay in that comfort zone of life. Don't stay in that limited environment. Don't limit yourself in a world filled with endless possibilities.

Who would you rather impress, them or the Master who gave you that idea that cannot be accomplished unless you step out to do it? Who are you going to give account to later for burying that idea or that gift locked up inside you, them or the Master?

In trying to accomplish great things, some people will not agree with your decisions. You might also not even succeed on your first attempt but try regardless. Failure is not final; it is a learning experience. It's simply telling you to try another approach. Keep trying even if you are terrified by the obstacles and the naysayers, but you must believe that you will succeed.

Would you say Apostle Peter failed, or did he accomplish something that none of the other disciples, or anyone else to date, have ever accomplished?

> *So, Peter went over the side of the boat and walked on the water toward Jesus. But when he saw the strong wind and the waves, he was terrified and began to sink. "Save me, Lord!" he shouted.*
>
> *Jesus immediately reached out and grabbed him. "You have so little faith," Jesus said. "Why did you doubt me?" (Matthew 14: 28-31 NLT)*

Peter's account informs us that when we set out to accomplish great things, we have to remove the fear element and be confident, keeping our eyes on the One who inspired us to do it. Sometimes you might even have to do it afraid, as Joyce Meyers would often say. The One who inspired you to step out and to do it cannot fail and neither will you if you trust him. Another scripture also says,

> *Commit your actions to the LORD,*
> *and your plans will succeed. Proverbs 16:3 (NLT)*

Maybe you got married and it never worked out, and your spouse served you divorce papers. What are you going to do now? Sit and cry, or move on to a better relationship? You might say that it is easier said than done. But regardless of your hypothesis, when someone wants to go and you don't move out of the way, you will get hurt and the person will still be gone. That's what happens to a number of people. They get hurt in the process because they refused to let go. Some never recover.

If you have ever lived in tropical countries such as the Caribbean or elsewhere that often experience hurricanes, then you would understand clearly what I am trying to say. When a hurricane is approaching, you know that you have to move out of its way and take cover. Why? Because whether you move out of its path or not, it will still pass through and create devastation. Consequently, physical death and life-threatening injuries are often sustained when people refuse to take cover. Same occurs in some relationships, if you do not take cover emotionally, physically, mentally and in other ways. You will be hurt and could even lose your life. Therefore, let go. Tomorrow, the sun will shine again.

Having said that, this statement reminds me of some great inspiration that we can draw from the elderly during a very difficult period.

During the height of the Coronavirus Pandemic, Captain Tom Moore defied the odds to walk around his house nearing the age of 100 years and raised nearly £38.9million. Consequently, he was knighted by the queen at Buckingham palace. Some of his favourite quotes were:

> *"Tomorrow will be a good day."*

> *"My today was all right and my tomorrow will certainly be better. That's the way I've always looked at life."*

> *'We will get through it.'*

Therefore, one has to learn to recognise when something is finished and move on from it because better is always ahead. Of course, there are times when things can be reconciled, and that should not be ruled out no matter how hopeless a situation may seem at times. Even with hurricanes, sometimes they change course or the weather predictions don't hold true.

Let me share a story:

I met Francis, a street preacher on the train. He was sharing his story before he got saved. He told of how he got married into a different culture. He said he loved his wife but she couldn't have children. His wife was a much older person and had a health condition. Francis didn't have the right to remain in the country, so he also got married to get his permanent leave to remain.

At the time of sharing his story, he was now a permanent resident. Soon after, he said he became unfaithful in the relationship and had a child with someone from his own nationality whilst still living with his wife. He told how he would often create quarrels with his wife, saying that he wanted children just to use that as an excuse to leave the house.

One day, he said he decided to move out, so he started packing and cursing in the process, telling his wife that he was leaving. He said his wife never said a word to him. Instead, she pulled up beside him in her wheelchair and started helping him pack. As he continued to pack his belongings, she would say to him, "Francis, here are some of my cutleries, you are going to need them to start out with. Here are some of my pots, you are going to need these too." So, she continued to list the items he would need and gave them to him.

Francis told how at that point, upon hearing her kind words and seeing the effort she was putting out to ensure that he would be equipped for wherever he was going, he said it broke his heart.

He said that he was so amazed because his wife never resisted him. She was helping him instead. He said, at that moment, her generosity confused him and he suddenly got convicted by his own behaviour. He told of how he couldn't believe what he was experiencing.

He said he had to unpack. That he stayed with her and took good care of her. He also took her out in her wheelchair without feeling embarrassed. That he wasn't ashamed to be with her any longer and he cared for her until she died.

Francis' wife understood what was happening and, in the end, her response taught him a great lesson. The natural thing was for her to resist him, but she didn't. She realised that she was facing a storm at that moment and, resisting it would only cause her more harm. Instead, like an eagle, she allowed it to lift her attitude and she soared above his behaviour. She acted contrary to what he was expecting, and it caused him to change his mind.

We are not supposed to be resisting every difficulty in life. Sometimes we need to make them be the lever that lifts us to new heights. Let that situation help you to emerge a better person. Let it teach others a lesson so that they too can use it to reflect and change for the better.

After Francis' wife died, he said he was in the process of changing his name to have a fresh start. I thought to myself at the time that it isn't a change of name that gives a person a fresh start. One has to change from within. It's a change of heart and mind that bring about real change.

As Francis moved on to a new life, I could envision him preaching this text on the train:

> *"I don't mean to say that I have already achieved these things or that I have already reached perfection. But I press on to possess that perfection for which Christ Jesus first possessed me. No, dear brothers and sisters, I have not achieved it, but I focus on this one thing: Forgetting the past and looking forward to what lies ahead, I press on to reach the end of the race and receive the heavenly prize for which God, through Christ Jesus, is calling us." (Philippians 3:12-14 NLT)*

One has to press on in order not to yield to temptations or revert to one's old ways in a new relationship. Yes, you can find the strength to move on, no matter what has happened in the past.

Remember, there are people at every stage of the journey trying to stop you from growing or moving on. Like Jesus's disciples who were trying to cross to the other side in their boat, and met the opposition of fierce storms. Don't be afraid when you face opposition, especially when you are trying to go to the other side in pursuit of your destiny. Like the boisterous waves trying to prevent the disciples from crossing, sometimes people, situations and things will try to create hindrances on your path to achieving your goals. However, you need to ignore, resist, persist, climb over and carry on regardless.

During one of the most difficult times in Great Britain when it was being bombed during the war years, Sir Winston Churchill told the people: *"Keep calm and carry on."* That's what we must all do amidst the adversities of life. Do not let it take you off course. Don't be afraid, just believe that you will overcome and you will. Remain positive. Keep your eyes on Jesus and on your goals when the going gets tough. Sometimes you need to become tough and get going despite the obstacles because even Jesus experienced the storms of life. Nonetheless, how he managed them made all the difference.

Jesus wasn't alarmed by storms. At times, he slept through them, and at other times, he rebuked them. This teaches us that we should know when to remain quiet in a situation and when to act. Knowing the difference is the prescription to many problems (Mark 4: 35-41 KJV).

How does one conquer the adversities of life and remain above situations? The answer lies in becoming resolute with the right focus. The scriptures below show us how:

Queen Esther said,

> *"I will go to the king, even though it is against the law. And if I perish, I perish." (Esther 4: 16 NIV)*

Also,

Shadrach, Meshach and Abednego replied to him, "King Nebuchadnezzar, we do not need to defend ourselves before you in this matter. If we are thrown into the blazing furnace, the God we serve is able to deliver us from it, and he will deliver us from Your Majesty's hand. But even if he does not, we want you to know, Your Majesty, that we will not serve your gods or worship the image of gold you have set up."
(Daniel 3: 16-18 NIV)

For those reasons, if things won't change, change things. It becomes easy by staying close to Jesus and putting your faith and trust in Him. Let Him be the captain of your ship, the source of your life, your confidant and the rest will be history.

If things won't change, change things.

11

FIGHT BACK

The first time I tasted marmite, I was very disappointed. "What a horrible taste!" I thought. Immediately, my mouth was filled with saliva, and I wanted to spit. I then thought, when life throws you a horrible taste, spit it out and move on. As a matter of fact, don't stop spitting until you are able to find the desired taste that pleases your taste buds.

On the contrary, some people would disagree with me because they are marmite lovers. People often say concerning marmite, it's either you love it or you loathe it. Many things in life are like marmite and the choice is yours, whether you want to accept and acquire the taste or reject by spitting it out. As our bishop would often say, "Whatever you don't resist, has the right to remain. Whatever you don't confront, you cannot conquer. Whatever you don't want, don't watch." If you pet a baby python or lion, you might end up becoming their meal in the future, so deal with situations before they deal with you. Fight back!

Some time ago, Allison and I were on our way to pick and eat strawberries on a farm, and to enjoy the ambience of a change of environment. We paid Uncle Tom, picked up our baskets and set off into the field. We couldn't wait to tuck into the strawberries as we competed like children to see who could find the biggest and ripest ones. We then shared them. They were sweet and juicy - the type that would definitely make you salivate.

After partially satisfying our crave, we sat on a concealed bench at the farthest end of the field, covered by laden, luscious passion fruit vines intertwined with twigs all around us. Only Uncle Tom knew that we were there. We could see others picking and tucking into their strawberries but they couldn't see us.

Occasionally, whilst talking, Allison and I would accidentally bite into a sour strawberry. It would set our teeth on edge, and immediately we would spit it out and try to replace the taste with another sweet and juicy one. Though, sometimes we didn't realise we had a whole bad batch and would have tasted several sour ones before we started to taste the sweet juicy ones again. Experts in strawberries often say, the brighter the colour, the sweeter the strawberry. But this sometimes doesn't hold true and it is the same with people. You cannot always judge a fruit or someone by outward appearance.

Sometimes, a person can be like a camouflaged predator, like the Orchid Mantis or the Walking Leaf insect that can destroy an entire vegetation. These insects mimic beautiful flowering plants but they are actually dangerous. For instance, the Orchid mantises are hostile insects. In spite of their flowery colours, they catch their prey by snatching it out of the air with their front legs and they devour it mercilessly. It is shocking to say, but in this 'international jungle' where we exist, there are a few human Orchid Mantis and Walking Leaves. People who behave in this way are what the bible refers to as wolves in sheep's clothing or Satan disguising himself as an angel of light.

Here you have to fight back. But how?

For instance, in a new relationship, watch how the person deals with disagreement or with a so-called enemy. It will be the same way that they will treat you. Likewise, if the person is trying to hit you, even as a joke. Maybe this is an indication that that strawberry is sour. Spit it out immediately. Spit out the abuse, don't settle for that taste. Spit out anger. Don't let it control you. Spit out low self-esteem, you are fearfully and wonderfully made. There is much more to you than what people can physically see. Therefore, spit out negativity, it will hinder the release of your potential and creativity. Spit out complaining. It will block your blessings.

When you begin to manage your mind and act, you will become more aware of the undesirables. Managing your mind and doing more is essential to fulfilling your potential in life. It involves spitting out all the other things that don't matter.

"Manage your mind and do more."

That's what the Lord once told me. I heard it clearly while I was boarding a train to work many years ago. Even now, it is still echoing in my ears because we can always do more if we try harder. In the process, this will increase your capacity.

To win in life, one has to fight back and it includes managing your mind and being more productive. Fighting can also take different forms depending on who your opponent is. It is a work of art done strategically under different circumstances. As simple as it sounds, it could be to simply manage your time, because success in life hinges on it. Therefore, you need to be ruthless with distractions. Some things are good in themselves, but if they are going to take you away from your goal or purpose in life, they are not good for you at that particular moment.

A heavy weight champion has to manage his mind and do more in the gym in order to retain his title. An artist has to keep working at the canvas to achieve perfection in order to have a competitive edge.

That's why what you think about is very important. You first win it or lose it in the mind before it is manifested. For instance, it's like saying you are going to ask your boss for a pay increase, although you know that you are not going to get it. That's a self-defeating thought.

That is why the scripture says,

> *"So, prepare your minds for action and exercise self-control." (1 Peter 1:13 NLT)*

You know that you can manage your mind and do more, hence, you can win in any situation. You can move from an unfavourable situation to a favourable one with the right mind-set, attitude and action. Therefore, there are endless possibilities because you have the mind of Christ. This means you have a wise, discerning and productive mind. The scripture says,

> *We have the mind of Christ. (1 Corinthians 2:16b)*

However, I believe if you don't manage your mind, negative thoughts will take up residence and derail you from the path to greatness. But there is always hope.

> *"For though the righteous fall seven times, they rise again." (Proverbs 24:16 NIV).*

It is always important to rise above the voices in your head. These include: voice of doubt, negativity, complaining, despair and the voice that says it cannot be done. Fight back using your faith. Fight back believing that you will overcome.

You will also hear other voices telling you to give up or give in, but it is during those difficult times that you need to begin to think like a winner. Announce to the contrary what you are hearing, feeling and experiencing. Accentuate the positives, the "I-can-do-all-things" mentality:

> *"I can do all things through Christ who strengthens me." (Philippians 4:13 NKJV)*

Rock the boat of your mind by stepping out into the water of faith-filled, positive self-talk and action. Visualize yourself overcoming situations and soaring to new heights. See yourself living the life that you want. See yourself in that new job role wearing your executive attire. Then begin to speak and act with confidence and gait like you are in the role, doing it. Words are creative, that is why God uses them. Words bring into existence what you would like to see.

> *"Then God said." (Genesis 1:3 NLT.)*

What have you been saying lately? Are you saying the right things? It is not only in saying, but in doing and doing it in the right way.

Then God said, "Let there be light," and there was light. (Genesis 1:3 NLT.)

It is important to note that prior to God saying that, everything was dark and hopeless. The scripture stated,

"The earth was formless and empty, and darkness covered the deep waters. And the Spirit of God was hovering over the surface of the waters." (Genesis 1: 2 NLT)

We know that anything the omnipotent God creates must be exceptionally beautiful and perfect, lacking nothing. Therefore, something must have tampered with His creation. However, I believe God drew our attention to it so that we could learn a lesson or two from this loss and devastation. He used it to demonstrate to us how to deal with challenges and not to give in, or give up, no matter how dark and hopeless things might appear to be. If we approach things with the right attitude, no matter what devastation the storms of life have brought us, we can still overcome. Another key point to note is that, although everything was empty and covered in darkness, God's spirit was still there hovering over the situation. The scripture stated:

"...And the Spirit of God was hovering over the surface of the waters." (Genesis 1: 2 NLT)

Hovering over simply means that God's spirit was elevated above the situation that he was experiencing. Likewise, you have God's spirit watching over you; living inside you; encircling you, and is right now going ahead of you. Therefore, you are elevated above every circumstance of life. As the scripture stated,

"For he raised us from the dead along with Christ and seated us with him in the heavenly realms because we are united with Christ Jesus." (Ephesians 2:6 NLT

If you view yourself in an elevated position regarding your circumstances then they lose the power to frustrate you, because you are above them. You also have God's Spirit living inside you to empower you to do as God did, and to get the same results or even greater. This is because, it is still God who is at work in you and will perform wonders through your faith. Then Jesus told them,

"I tell you the truth, anyone who believes in me will do the same works I have done, and even greater works, because I am going to be with the Father. You can ask for anything in my name, and I will do it, so that the Son can bring glory to the Father. Yes, ask me for anything in my name, and I will do it! (John 14:12-14 NLT)

Allison, all you need to do now is to believe. Have faith that your situation will change. That is why the scriptures said we are to fight the good fight of faith. Faith is a fight but a good one.

What is faith? Faith is having complete trust and confidence in God regarding the things we hope for, although they have not yet materialised. That is why you have to fight to keep your hope and expectations alive because God cannot fail. God and his Word are one.

"In the beginning was the Word, and the Word was with God, and the Word was God." (John 1:1 KJV).

God speaks mainly through his Word and God has the final say. Therefore, whatever his Word says about your situation will definitely come to pass. For the scripture states:

> *"I tell you the truth, until heaven and earth disappear, not even the smallest detail of God's law will disappear until its purpose is achieved." (Matthew 5:18 NLT)*

If God's Word says you are more than a conqueror, you are, and because of that, you cannot lose any battle. King David didn't lose any battle during his lifetime because of the God factor in his life, including the wisdom to consult God before making a decision.

You cannot fight back and win without wise actions. Part of being wise is to listen to advice and instructions from God and others. "Commit your actions to the Lord and your plans will succeed." (Proverbs 16:3 NLT)

Also, it is written: "Where there is no counsel, the people fall; but in the multitude of counsellors there is safety." (Proverbs 11:14 NKJV)

Having said that, there are no circumstances that can come against you and defeat you, because the Greater One lives in you.

> *You are of God, little children, and have overcome them, because He who is in you is greater than he who is in the world. (1 John 4:4 NKJV).*

You also need to believe in yourself and have the confidence that:

"I can do all things through Christ who strengthens me." (NKJV)

Consequently, don't settle for second best when God has the very best for you. Don't settle for Esau when God is preparing you for your Isaac. Don't live in despair. Don't settle for an empty life due to losses and devastation. God didn't settle for it either in Genesis chapter one. God fought back by speaking what He wanted to see manifested and so should you because the bible states;

> *I say, 'You are gods;*
> *you are all children of the Most High. (Psalms 82:6*
> *NLT)*

As children of the Most High God, we should operate like Him and use our words to change our situation. Speaking God's Word into your situation coupled with believing it, is a simple effective tool to recover what was lost, stolen or to bring something into existence. That is why Jesus said:

> *It is the Spirit who gives life; the flesh profits nothing.*
> *The words that I speak to you are spirit, and they are*
> *life. But there are some of you who do not*
> *believe." (John 6:63-64 NKJV)*

For God's word to work in your life, you must believe. There is no other way around it. If you are a critic, it will not work for you. You have to adopt childlike faith and believe.

> *But without faith it is impossible to please Him, for*
> *he who comes to God must believe that He is,*
> *and that He is a rewarder of those who diligently*
> *seek Him. (Hebrews 11:6 NKJV)*

Most importantly, you need to follow God's instructions. He can speak to you in several ways such as: through His Word, through a person or through dreams amongst others.

> *But his mother told the servants, "Do whatever he tells you."*

This is key to the manifestation of God's word in your life – doing whatever he tells you to do. Obedience is a winning strategy if you are to fight back and win. Is it always easy? No. But you will always see the fruits of your obedience. Because the scripture stated:

> *"For the word of God is living and powerful, and sharper than any two-edged sword, piercing even to the division of soul and spirit, and of joints and marrow, and is a discerner of the thoughts and intents of the heart." (Hebrews 4:12 NKJV)*

Words have power. Begin to speak God's Word and your desires. As you speak, begin to visualize their manifestation. It's a fight-back strategy. As it is written,

> *".... God, who gives life to the dead and calls those things which do not exist as though they did." (Romans 4:17 NKJV.)*

Situations and things will start to change when you change the way you view and approach them. If you believe, they will manifest. If you don't, they won't.

Therefore, never give up!

> *"For there is hope for a tree, if it is cut down, that it will sprout again, and that its tender shoots will not cease." (Job 14:7 NKJV)*

Jesus also said,

> *"These things I have spoken unto you, that in me ye might have peace. In the world ye shall have tribulation: but be of good cheer; I have overcome the world." (John 16:33 KJV).*

Because Jesus overcame, you also will overcome. His Spirit is at work within you.

Expect to see and experience sunshine again because, like the shifting of the clouds, a shift is coming to your life. It's only a matter of time. The gloom will soon disappear and you will see and experience the warmth of the sun's rays again.

You will experience joy again. You will experience peace, spiritual prosperity, financial prosperity, marital prosperity, relational prosperity, prosperity in your health and businesses, your children will prosper and you will prosper in all that pertains to you. All round favour, blessings and glory will be your portion in Jesus name. It is no wonder the scripture says:

> "Beloved, I wish above all things that thou mayest prosper and be in health, even as thy soul prospereth." (3 John 1:2 KJV)

Mary and Martha lost hope because Jesus didn't turn up when they expected him to.

Are you losing hope, thinking that it is impossible at this late stage for your situation to change?

Martha said to Him, "I know that he will rise again in the resurrection at the last day."

Jesus said to her, "I am the resurrection and the life. He who believes in Me, though he may die, he shall live. And whoever lives and believes in Me shall never die. Do you believe this? (John 11:24-26 NKJV)

Like Martha, Jesus is asking you the same question concerning your situation. Do you believe that Jesus is the resurrection and the life?

Do you believe Jesus can change your hopeless situation?

Life is a fight. Faith is also a fight against doubt and unbelief. That's why the scripture encourages us to:

"Fight the good fight of faith..." (1 Timothy 6:12 NKJV)

Believe that you can begin again. Believe that you can achieve in one year or less what would take a decade or lifetime for someone else to achieve. Believe that God can fast-track your situation thereby making up for lost opportunities, lost time, lost resources, lost favour and glory.

In the scripture, God told us through the prophet Isaiah that:

I will answer them before they even call to me.

While they are still talking about their needs,

I will go ahead and answer their prayers! (Isaiah 65:24 NLT)

God knows our thoughts and our heart's desire. He is saying, even before you ask, I will answer and while you are still talking about it, I will give it to you.

When I began my current employment several years ago, I started out as an agency staff. At the time, I had just returned from a short, failed mission abroad. I felt like a failure because things didn't turn out as expected. I felt like a deflated balloon. I was in a lot of pain and grief. I felt hopeless, ashamed and foolish. I felt like my whole life had been wasted and I didn't have anyone to turn to who could help in a real, tangible way.

I was also very broke. Consequently, I was trying to re-settle into permanent employment. I received a temporary agency post. However, I liked it and began to envision myself working permanently in that institution.

It so happened that Jane, who I was covering for, was on sick leave suffering from cancer. At the time, I met Jane only once in order to do the change-over of roles, but hadn't learned of the extent of her illness then. Although still hurting from my own experience, as soon as I learnt of Jane's situation, I tried to dry my tears and genuinely began praying for her to get well. I also invited the church to pray.

One day, whilst reflecting on the temporary post that I was in at work, I observed that there was an extra desk in the office that was not occupied. I didn't even notice it at first because people would often use it from time to time but it didn't belong to anyone. It was vacant.

When I observed this vacant desk, I had the urge to pray about it. Later, it came to my mind to ask the Lord to create a permanent post for me in order to fill that vacant desk. Then on a regular basis I would pray. Each time, I reminded the Lord that there was room enough in that department for me, because an empty desk was there to be filled. I kept praying:

> *"Lord, create a permanent post for me, and heal Jane."*

Since I was usually the first person to get into the office, each morning I would pray and envisioned the empty desk as my own. So, I would look at it and say:

> *"Lord, create a permanent post for me, and heal Jane."*

During this time, the secretary would call me from time to time to tell me that the organisation was very pleased with my performance. Also, that they would like to keep me, but there was no vacancy as Jane was still in post. Despite knowing these facts, I kept praying:

> *"Lord, create a permanent post for me, and heal Jane."*

Facts are based on evidence and can be proven. But I know that it was not the truth. Truth is anchored in belief. Truth is in a higher realm. The fact that there was an empty desk with no vacancy to fill it, doesn't mean that it could not be filled. The truth is, if I believe that a vacancy exists for me, then my faith in God could make it come true, thereby making it a reality. In the meantime, in the department, the manager would often tell me how I made her job easy for her.

Looking back now, one might think that the two prayers were contradictory because, if Jane was healed and returned to her post, I would have to leave the organisation. Nevertheless, with the eye of faith, I wasn't asking for Jane's post. I saw the vacant desk and wanted the Lord to *create* a post for me to fill. I also believed God could do it, if it was his perfect will because his Word is infallible.

> *"I am the LORD, the God of all the peoples of the world. Is anything too hard for me? (Jeremiah 32:27 NLT).*

Maybe another person would have prayed for Jane not to return to work so that they could get her post, but not me. Because, I knew that would be evil and my prayers would not get answered.

> *"And even when you ask, you don't get it because your motives are all wrong…" (James 4:3 NLT)*

I also knew I serve a God that nothing is impossible for him to do. Additionally, He is a creative God who isn't just able to create a way, but he is also The Way. Therefore, I began to observe and meditate on the following scriptures to justify my request:

> *"I am the LORD, the God of all mankind. Is anything too hard for me?" (Jeremiah 32: 27 KJV)*

> *Thus, saith the LORD, which maketh a way in the sea, and a path in the mighty waters; (Isaiah 43:16 KJV)*

> *Jesus saith unto him, I am the way, the truth, and the life: (John 14:6 KJV)*

During that time, I could picture Jane coming back to her post, and at the same time, me occupying the vacant desk beside her. I believed in my heart that God could create a vacancy and He did. At the time, I kept working hard. I didn't even work like an agency staff. I stayed back late, arrived early and kept working to a high standard and with much enthusiasm. In the process, my manager continued to tell me how I made her job easy for her.

I joined the organization in January. Within four months, whilst Jane was still away on sick leave, my manager informed us in one of our department meetings that the head of the institution was going to expand our department. My manager used these very words, "The principal said that she was going to create a new post in our department." Up to that point and even to date, I never told anyone about my prayers. When she told us that a new post would be created, the expression *'created'* resonated with me because that's the exact word I used in my prayers. I had asked God to create a permanent post for me and that was exactly what He did.

They advertised. I applied for the post, competed with others and got it. I was elated. I had succeeded. God did it. He created the post for me. *As the scripture stated,*

> *"...God creates new things out of nothing." (Romans 4:17 NLT).*

I was amazed at how quickly that answer came. Within four months, I was made permanent. Jane was also well enough to return to her post. God had answered both prayer points. What if I didn't speak and declared what I wanted? Maybe nothing would have happened. For every action, there is usually a reaction. No action, nothing in motion, no reaction. So, I literally prayed and spoke the permanent post into existence.

The fact is, there was no evidence of a physical vacancy. But the truth is, the potential was there for it to be created and God's word brought it into existence. As the scripture says,

> *"Imitate God, therefore, in everything you do, because you are his dear children." (Ephesians 5:1 NLT).*

> *"And God said, let there be light: and there was light." (Genesis 1:3 KJV)*

I imitated what God did and the same happened for me too. For I said: *"Lord, create a permanent post for me and heal Jane."* And that's what happened. A new post was created for me and Jane returned to work. I said it and there it was. I am still operating in that reality now. Glory be to God.

But it didn't end there. Surprisingly, within a month of getting the permanent post, my manager informed us that she was leaving the organisation. We broke for summer holidays shortly after. The first day we resumed work, one of the assistant principals said to me that they had a meeting during the holiday break, and everyone agreed that I was the ideal candidate for the managerial post. However, because they didn't want me to decline the post; they decided to wait until I returned after the holidays to ask me whether I would be willing to assume the responsibility. As soon as he had finished speaking to me, I accepted. The principal then came over to the department and verbally announced a new pay package for me, and the rest is history, as the saying goes.

I was amazed. Before I could start the permanent post that I had prayed for, I was quickly transitioned into a higher, new role unexpectedly. So, Jane returned to work to find me as her new boss. Amazing! I was not sitting at her desk anymore. I was now at the manager's desk. You could see her facial expression. I wasn't sure how to interpret it. She must have been extremely stunned by my quick transition. God works in mysterious ways. He performs wonders. It reminded me of this scripture:

> *Yes indeed, it won't be long now."* GOD's *Decree.*
>
> *"Things are going to happen so fast your head will swim, one thing fast on the heels of the other. You won't be able to keep up. Everything will be happening at once—and everywhere you look, blessings! Blessings like wine pouring off the mountains and hills. (Amos 9:13 MSG).*

That's what happens when you pray for yourself and others. I pray it will happen for you too.

It is now years later, and I am still managing the department. Now I am looking forward to moving on to even better things. When you obey the commands of the Lord, the scripture says,

> *"The* LORD *will make you the head and not the tail, and you will always be on top and never at the bottom." (Deuteronomy 28:13 NLT).*

God is a God of amazing surprises. However, I also believe God prepares us in advance even for things we didn't pray for. I said this because, during that same summer holiday, prior to receiving this managerial post that I never applied for, I accompanied a church group up a mountain to pray. In between intervals, whilst praying and worshipping, the overseeing minister would single people out and prophesy into their lives. It so happened that he singled me out too, and simply said to me:

> *"I can see something coming your way, and I can see you reach out and grab it."*

It turned out to be what I did. He said it about two weeks before I returned to work after the holidays, and that's exactly what happened. One of the assistant principals spoke to me about the post and I never hesitated to accept or "grab it." It therefore meant that the same day that I started my new permanent post, that's the very same day I was thrust into another new and higher role and my pay package changed immediately - just like that. I didn't even apply for the role. The blessings began flooding in because I was at the right place at the right time. As the scripture states,

> *"The steps of a good man are ordered by the LORD, And He delights in his way." (Psalm 37:23 NKJV).*

Despite the constant reminder that there were no vacancies, unknowing to me, God had already ordered my steps at that employment via that agency because he knew what he would do. Through divine providence, a way was created. God did a new thing right there and then. For God had said:

> *"Behold, I will do a new thing, now it shall spring forth;*
> *Shall you not know it?*
> *I will even make a road in the wilderness*
> *And rivers in the desert. (Isaiah 43:19 NKJV)*

What are you asking the Lord for? Does it seem impossible?

Pray! Speak! Fast! Sing! Give thanks! Meditate! Whatever you do, you must believe and it shall be done, providing it is God's will. Even before the answer comes, be joyful about it and give thanks. Thanksgiving with a good attitude will release and perfect your answer.

> *Therefore, with joy you will draw water from the wells of salvation. (Isaiah 12:3 NKJV)*

Therefore, ask big. Ask genuinely. Ask with confidence and with good motives. Ask for that which will not only benefit you and your family, but also your neighbours and society at large. Then you know your desires will be granted. Ask so that when you receive, you can also be an answer to the prayers of others. God knows your needs and desires, but He still wants you to come to Him and make your request known. Are you asking? Are you seeking? Are you knocking? For the scriptures said:

> *Ask, and it will be given to you; seek, and you will find; knock, and it will be opened to you. For everyone who asks receives, and he who seeks finds, and to him who knocks it will be opened. Or what man is there among you who, if his son asks for bread, will give him a stone? Or if he asks for a fish, will he give him a serpent? If you then, being evil, know how to give good gifts to your children, how much more will your Father who is in heaven give good things to those who ask Him! (Matthew 7: 7-11 NKJV)*

Asking is a fight-back strategy in order to claim what belongs to you. The scripture reminds us that: *"You don't have what you want because you don't ask God for it." (James 4:2 NLT)*

Jesus also said:

> *Therefore, I say to you, whatever things you ask when you pray, believe that you receive them, and you will have them. (Mark 11:24 KJV)*

Always look for opportunities in every difficulty. Believe that you will find them, then take advantage of them. Fight back by taking action.
God is waiting to surprise you.

12

LIFE CHANGING EXPERIENCES

If Allison thought she was the only one facing life's challenges, she should think again.

I met Doggy some time ago whilst doing evangelism and he told of how he had four children. They were his hope for living, he said. At the time of speaking to him, he was coming out of a local newsagent store with a pint of lager. He told me how he used to be a heroin addict. He had all sorts of piercings on his skin to show for it, and one was even infected, with pus oozing from it. Adding to that, he had been to prison countless times. Now, he had taken up drinking because he found that it replaced the urge to take heroin. He said he felt very accomplished taking up this new habit of drinking as he believed it was much better than taking heroin. However, he didn't realise that he was still trapped.

I encouraged and prayed for him on the spot. He was very receptive and hopeful. He added that he still prays the rosary amongst his friends who were often amazed. He even showed me a crucifix tattooed on his chest. I prayed for him that the crucifix would not just be an outward expression of his faith; but it would become an inward expression soon, so that he could experience complete deliverance from his addictions.

Although trapped, Doggy was upbeat, personable and appreciative of life. His attitude was second to none. I was amazed. I ran into him on a few other occasions and he was still filled with gratitude for life despite struggling to give up his addiction. I kept praying for him because prayer is limitless where physical help fails to reach. I can envision him getting delivered and moving on to fulfil his destiny in life like many others have done.

We were all created differently, each with our individual gifts, and we need to find expression for it. It is people like Doggy, who are usually written off by society, who often make the greatest come-back in life, if targeted support is given. As a people, in this global economy, each of us matter. It is no wonder certain resources are found in particular parts of the world, and in other parts, they simply don't exist so that trade could bring us together.

I later met Marcus through evangelism. He encouraged me in my effort and told how he had become 'born again' and had been growing in his faith. He then recounted part of his life's story to me. He told how he got caught up in a gang and had to run for his life to a different part of the country. He told how he managed to throw a few items of clothing into a small suitcase and flee with minimal cash. He then said that the only real asset he had at the time was his trade as a plumber. Then, one night, he got saved whilst carrying two pints of lager in his hands. Since then, he never went back to drinking. He is still amazed by the transformation.

Just before speaking to me, I watched him park an expensive jeep at the train station. He said he chose to spend a few minutes with me recounting what the Lord had done for him. He had also acquired a lovely home which he still couldn't believe he was able to achieve at the age of 35. At the time, he was also in the process of getting married and he was extremely excited about it. Therefore, never write anyone off. With the right help and support, anyone can become a better person and achieve their goals in life.

As a society, we should aspire to function like the different organs in our bodies. Although different, yet connected in order for our bodies to operate at optimal efficiency. If our eyes should say they are going to stop working, then there would be no light for our bodies. If our hearts should join the eyes in not functioning, then the whole body would cease to function. We therefore need to find our part in the body of Christ and play it well in order to have a more effective and productive society. The less adored organs also play a vital role and should be cared for very well because the body simply cannot function without them. Likewise, we should offer help to people who often struggle to help themselves. When they are being cared for and given the opportunity to fulfil their purpose, our society would be much more productive, healthy and peaceful. The crime rate would also be lower.

Like Doggy and Marcus, I also listened to Spark's testimony. He told how, as a teenager, he got caught up in gang warfare in London after his parents were separated. He blamed his mother for the separation and his waywardness got worse. He said he used to stab his victims and often received the same in reprisal. He showed some of the healed wounds on his arms and legs. He went on to say that the reason he stabbed his victims was because he liked to see and smell blood. He was fascinated by it, he said.

At the time, he was sharing his story at a large gathering to encourage other youths to choose a better path. At this point, he was completely transformed and was in his fourth year at a medical school in London, studying to become a brain surgeon. Sometimes people's destinies are diverted and it was divine that he was delivered and found the right expression for his gift.

He was supposed to be a brain surgeon operating on people's heads to save their lives, but look how he got started? He was stabbing his victims because he liked the sight and scent of blood. Thank God he found the correct expression for his gift.

It is the humanitarian work that we do that helps to get people like Spark back on track in life. Since his testimony, the last update I had about him was that he had graduated and was working as a successful brain surgeon in a leading London hospital.

In relating synopses of these individuals' lives, I am being reminded from the Great Book of Instruction:

"Just as our bodies have many parts and each part has a special function, so it is with Christ's body. We are many parts of one body, and we all belong to each other. In his grace, God has given us different gifts for doing certain things well. So, if God has given you the ability to prophesy, speak out with as much faith as God has given you. If your gift is serving others, serve them well. If you are a teacher, teach well. If your gift is to encourage others, be encouraging. If it is giving, give generously. If God has given you leadership ability, take the responsibility seriously. And if you have a gift for showing kindness to others, do it gladly. Don't just pretend to love others. Really love them." (Romans 12:4-9 NLT)

We should help each other to discover our gifts and function in it. That's where the difference comes in. Spark would have been one brain surgeon short in his field, if he had died in gang warfare. That is why we are called to make a difference, and it doesn't matter what you do. The farmer is just as important too. If he doesn't go to work, the nation dies because we cannot survive without food. Similarly, if the cleaner doesn't turn up to work, the hygiene of that place would go bad, leading to the spread of infections and diseases. So, it's vital that each of us play our role in life. We are individuals, but together we function better —as a family unit, as a group, as a community and as a society in general. When one-part hurts, the rest of the body should also feel the pain because it is inter-connected. Hence, we should be kinder to each other.

Have you ever noticed when a foreign object gets into one of your eyes that the other eye is equally teary as well? It's because they are meant to work together. That is why multi-disciplinary collaboration is promoted in health and social care so that vital signs regarding patients' diagnosis and care are not missed. This is enhanced through better communication and a wider field of expertise from which to consult. Therefore, whether one is a professional or informal carer, we are all better working together.

That's what we do at Charity Odyssey. We work as a team, because we believe that we are better together. I came to realise that my purpose was in my career. It was not just to carry out successful surgeries, but to administer care and restore dignity to lives.

Dr Carey: Elsie, as a retired surgeon, I often thought about the brevity of life, especially when we were not able to save a few patients in surgery. Additionally, there's the countless number of lives being lost on the streets each day due to violence or other circumstances. Having said that, the other day I was thinking about eternity, and I was intrigued by it. It can also be frightening if you are a bit unsure about it.

Let's face it. Whether one believes in eternity or not, the fact is, it does exist. There is life after death, and it does matter where you will spend it. The probability that we will all die one day, is one. Then after death, comes judgment. Then eternity follows. Eternity is where you will live permanently, forever. However, the beauty of life is that you own that decision. You can get to choose where you want to live forever now, whilst you are alive. It's a spiritual investment for your future. The choice to serve Christ in spirit and in truth will secure your eternity in heaven. As the following scriptures say:

> *"I call heaven and earth as witnesses today against you, that I have set before you life and death, blessing and cursing; therefore, choose life, that both you and your descendants may live;" (Deuteronomy 30:19 NKJV)*

> *Jesus said to him, "I am the way, the truth, and the life. No one comes to the Father except through Me." (John 14:6 NKJV)*

> *"Enter by the narrow gate; for wide is the gate and broad is the way that leads to destruction, and there are many who go in by it. Because narrow is the gate*

*and difficult is the way which leads to life, and there
are few who find it." (Matthew 7:13-14 NKJV)*

I have also come to realise that your talent, including your work can continue to impact lives long after you are gone. It will also follow you into eternity. So, it is important to discover and manifest them in order to benefit others and bring glory to your creator. Don't bury your talent. It's equivalent to wasting your life. Discover, develop and deploy it instead.

"So, he who had received five talents came and brought five other talents, saying, 'Lord, you delivered to me five talents; look, I have gained five more talents besides them.' His lord said to him, 'Well done, good and faithful servant; you were faithful over a few things, I will make you ruler over many things. Enter into the joy of your lord.' (Matthew 25:20-21 NKJV)

The book of the Acts of the Apostles contains the life, work, faith and good deeds of those who have long gone before us. However, they have left room for us to emulate them today. That is why wealthy individuals often set up foundations etc. Some have written books and have left great sermons that keep impacting lives even today. You should let your gifts, work and good deeds serve as a library for others to tap into and benefit from, even after you are gone. Consequently, we must be careful how we live our lives, because indeed, our work and good deeds will follow us. As it is written,

*"And I heard a voice from heaven saying, "Write this
down: Blessed are those who die in the Lord from now
on. Yes, says the Spirit, they are blessed indeed, for*

they will rest from their hard work; for their good deeds follow them!" (Revelation 14:13 NLT).

Therefore, it is important to engage meaningfully in life and make a difference. It is not always easy to balance one's time, but we need to try to do so in order to keep on doing good deeds, persevere in faith and trust God.

Love for God and humanity should be the driving force behind our pursuit in life, guiding us as we fulfil our destinies and impact communities and nations. Like the stars in the galaxies, keep your candle lit. Never let it go out. As the scripture states:

> *"You are the light of the world. A city that is set on a hill cannot be hidden. Nor do they light a lamp and put it under a basket, but on a lampstand, and it gives light to all who are in the house.*
>
> *Let your light so shine before men, that they may see your good works and glorify your Father in heaven."*
> *(Matthew 5:14-16 NKJV)*

Elsie: Dr Carey, I believe you heard right when you decided to undertake this charity initiative. You are playing the role very well. You are a man of faith and good works, and that's why you and your organisation are unstoppable.

Dr Carey: Elsie, I would like this charity to become a foundation, to continue long after its members. As a team, we would like to keep touching lives. When people come to our office, no matter how dead their situation might seem, like that of Lazarus, we believe that God's glory can be restored in their lives. We believe that transformation can take place even if some of them don't have the capacity to believe for themselves. Some of the people we meet are so emotionally and psychologically damaged, or even dead due to the trauma they experienced, but there is always hope of a resurrection.

Sometimes we have to believe on their behalf. We believe that all things are possible. If their situation seemed dead and stinking like that of Lazarus, we know that we have to intercede and do the believing for them. We have to initiate action on their behalf through faith, prayer and counselling in pursuit of their deliverance until they get on board with us. We have to inspire them to rise up and act by putting into practice what we try to teach them.

Some of these candidates, on their own, would never get employed because many have criminal records. Therefore, resurrection sometimes comes in the form of us sourcing the job for them. More importantly, helping them to create their own employment. Like Lazarus who was just on the receiving end and could do nothing about his situation, so are some of our candidates. We have to do everything for them in order to restore them, so that they can in turn start doing things for themselves, thereby giving them another chance in life.

Others who are in dire situations but, not completely hopeless, are encouraged to believe that their situation can change. If they believe and are willing to participate, we then begin to instil courage in them to believe in themselves. We also train them in how to master job interviews and acquire new skills set to release their potential. For each and every one of them, no matter how embarrassing or stinky their situation might seem, we want to see miracles take place in their lives. We want to see a resurrected new life resulting in wholeness and new lifestyles. Jesus intervened in Lazarus' hopeless situation and completely restored him back to life. We are imitators of Jesus, so we believe we can make a difference through Jesus Christ at work in each of us.

We have seen in the scriptures where, due to fear of raiders, a man's burial had to be rushed. He was hurriedly thrown into the Prophet Elisha's grave and, when the dead body came into contact with Elisha's bones, the man came back to life. Like that man, many of our candidates have been thrown in hurriedly in desperation through our doors at Charity Odyssey by life's circumstances. We also believe that they too will experience a resurrection when they come into contact with us. They too will experience the miraculous, a complete turnaround of their situations; thereby jumping back to their feet totally restored. As seen from the following scripture:

> *"Then Elisha died and they buried him.*
>
> *Sometime later, raiding bands of Moabites, as they often did, invaded the country. One day, some men were burying a man and spotted the raiders. They threw the man into Elisha's tomb and got away. When the body touched Elisha's bones, the man came alive, stood up, and walked out on his own two feet. (2 Kings 13: 20-21 MSG).*

That's what we want to see happen to people as they step into our offices at Charity Odyssey. We want them to be revived, get back on their feet and walk out of their dead or hopeless situations. I want this organisation to have the same resurrection impact like what happened to that man that was thrown into Elijah's tomb.

Sometimes life's circumstances have thrown many people into the graves of life. Many people are buried in life due to varying situations, but because we believe in the risen Christ, our Lord and Saviour, we believe we are able to pattern the work that He has already done. So, we allow Him to work through us. We will never take credit for anything, because it is Christ at work in and through us. Without His hands in our lives and work, everything would be futile. Therefore, I am encouraged when I read another scripture which says,

> *"I tell you the truth, anyone who believes in me will do the same works I have done, and even greater works, because I am going to be with the Father. You can ask for anything in my name, and I will do it, so that the Son can bring glory to the Father. Yes, ask me for anything in my name, and I will do it!" (John 14:12-14 NLT)*

That's what we at Charity Odyssey have been doing. We have been praying, working and believing that lives will be transformed on a daily basis as they come into contact with us. That is why we still believe that no matter how hopeless or dead a situation might seem, it can be resurrected. Thus, we always speak life into every circumstance by asking God to do the miraculous through us. Additionally, we always try to keep our hopes alive irrespective of the circumstances.

Always look at the bright side of life. That's where Jesus is located, because He is light. He is life. He is the truth. And the truth is, there is always hope of a resurrection. There is always hope of making a come-back in life. There is always hope for anyone who is still alive, even if their situation seems dead. That is why the scripture says,

"Anyone who is among the living has hope - even a live dog is better off than a dead lion!" (Ecclesiastes 9:4 NIV).

At Charity Odyssey, we always try to accentuate the positives, and it is no wonder we are seeing many lives being transformed with accompanying great results and testimonies. That's part of living life to its fullest – doing practical things to see the lives of others transformed for the better.

Our hope is to see people everywhere being stirred with joy and confidence to do great exploits. We want to see broken families mended. We want to see people creating their own businesses and becoming employers. We want to see people settled into jobs and getting promoted. We want to see people being prayed for, get healed and come to faith in Christ. We want to see people being the hands and feet of Jesus. We want to see people expressing the mind and attitude of Christ in how they treat and relate to others.

However, we have to start the process by holding their hands, offering support and guidance to make this and even more become possible. It is our hope that, by doing this, things will replicate and have the kind of domino effect whereby other people's lives will be positively impacted by each other.

Dr Carey (Continued): Like a potter with his clay jars, I can see people through similar lenses on a daily basis. As I look, I see many broken lives like broken vessels. Many with cracks and chips. Many with faded colours, looking dull and unattractive due to the wear and tear of life. Still others have something missing such as a handle or base due to physical, emotional and psychological trauma. We want to reach out and touch them. We want to introduce them to Christ, the Great Potter who will restore them holistically to their original design. Christ's love is gentle and kind. He restores, refines and redecorates lives. He will put His protective shield on them and place them in His display cabinet for all to see. They will become treasures and trophies of great value - a rare collection of His creation. These people will then rediscover their true value. They will also be valued and respected by others, because the Great Potter has remoulded and rebranded them. Let Christ remould and rebrand you today.

Many people are hurting, and some are abandoned and left for dead, like Rocky. We want to be an extension of the Potter's hands in offering practical help in every way. We want to take them in at Charity Odyssey and allow the Master Potter to restore them. To restore what has been damaged, broken and lost. I often remember my old high school motto written in Latin: "Facto Non Verba" which translates to mean, "Deeds not words." We believe it's by doing that we can make a difference in the lives of others, thereby getting them back on track.

Elsie: Woah! Doc. That's incredible indeed! I believe your message should reach a wider audience. Young people and the retired would be motivated to volunteer at Charity Odyssey. You also need to document your ideas into a book. You made me want to quit my full-time job to volunteer at your organization. The only obstacle is, I have a family with two young children to raise, so I need to continue earning.

Dr Carey: Elsie, I do speak about it frequently. We also have a forum where most of what I am saying to you, is being aired on weekdays. There is also a programme on Chill FM every

Wednesday and Friday between 6pm and 7pm called "The Meaning of Life." It's a series. I am one of the presenters and it's a great forum that helps to accentuate the work that we do at Charity Odyssey. It also helps us to get others involved in supporting our mission.

The aim is to impact communities so that youths, the disadvantaged, the elderly and those who have lost their way can be recalibrated and transformed through the support they receive from us in order to live a better life. We want to help them so that they can in turn, help themselves and others. If each one helps the other, the sky would be the limit to what we could accomplish. The opportunities would also be endless. As a nation, we would be unstoppable, like the people who were building the tower of Babel. Only God could stop them. *(Genesis 11:1-8 NIV)*.

As humans, we should always work to achieve something so great that only God can stop us. We also know that providing the intention is good, God will not stop us. He would instead be super impressed by our fruit-bearing initiative. That is what we at Charity Odyssey aim to do. As long as there is a precedent for it, the possibilities are endless. We can also set our own precedents by using God's creative wisdom thereby leaving a trail on the journey of life for others to follow. We can always do greater works because of Jesus.

Dr Carey: (Continued.) Elsie, although salary is important, it is not what drives what we do. None of us at the charity receive a salary. We are all volunteers. We do it sacrificially, and from our hearts, because we are passionate to see lives changed. That is one of the reasons we are so respected by many of our donors when they see our accounting audit.

Actually, you couldn't put a price tag on what we do. It's priceless. In time, you will come to realise that as people mature, they begin to view life through a different set of lenses.

When individuals are young, there is a desire to create a style of living and to ensure that they achieve all the 'toys' of life in making that possible. As one begins to mature, one tends to pay less attention to the extrinsic values of material things like brand-name cars, real estates including luxury homes, and even money. These things don't really bring real joy or satisfaction. The things that make people self-actualise and bring real great intrinsic rewards are often not self-centred but people-centred. Amongst such things are: opening up an orphanage to transform the lives of the poor; writing a book to inspire others to acquire good values; opening up a rehabilitation centre; creating employment for people; feeding the poor with hot meals every day and equipping people with new skills set to earn a living for themselves.

If your goals are self-driven, you might tend to become selfish in your pursuit in life. If they are people driven, they will be community centred. When they are community centred, you will gain a higher level of intrinsic satisfaction. Therefore, your focus should be centred on the intrinsic value to be gained from helping people in your community and internationally so that you can live a rich and satisfied life. For instance, hearing of people suffering in a third-world country from cataracts that can so easily be cured, via helping them through a mission's trip. Children who are being excluded from school every day because of the inability to afford school fees or even basic hygiene kits, is a tragedy of life. Bringing treatment to restore their sight and finance their education would bring much more intrinsic satisfaction.

It is a feeling that is totally different from showing up in a Rolls Royce at a party trying to impress some jealous friends who don't even care much about your well-being. The satisfaction you get from helping to transform lives is indescribable and life-changing. It will inspire you in wanting to leave your own trail in this jungle called life too. Most importantly, you will be blessed by the Creator of life.

Elsie (Listening and thinking to herself): You can say all that Dr Carey. You are retired and have already accumulated your "toys." You are now trying to self-actualise. That's why you can view life from that perspective. Maybe my values are a bit twisted at the moment, but I need cash to care. I need to accumulate my own "toys" first, then I can emulate you. I need cash to keep my two young children in private school and to live a better life. Maybe I need to grow more in terms of my outlook on life but that's my reality right now. Maybe I am a cynic in some sense or maybe not. I think I am just a realist. Whatever it is, I am honest with myself.

Elsie: Dr Carey, you are like a great vintage wine at our dinner table during Christmas. You have matured with age and experience. I need to borrow some of your experience and expertise so that I can emulate you. I would like to have your level of love and compassion for people. I have not seen many people like you, and your team who care for others so genuinely and selflessly.

Dr Carey (Blushed): "Have you made your choice yet, Elsie? One file seems to have caught your attention for a long time now. Who is that person you are scrutinizing?"

Elsie: I nearly forgot that I was selecting a candidate because you had me hooked on listening to you. Your words simultaneously inspired and pierced my heart like a dagger. I felt inspired, challenged and at a time condemned within myself. I must admit, I need more compassion and love for humanity. Now I am feeling that I need to do much more to care, and you have certainly inspired me in wanting to do much more for the candidate that we are about to hire.

Listening to you just now, I am beginning to look at life in a completely new way, although, to be honest with you, something inside me is telling me to think "toys" first, before people. It's a struggle at times, Dr Carey. No wonder one of the apostles in scriptures said,

> *"I have discovered this principle of life—that when I want to do what is right, I inevitably do what is wrong." (Romans 7:21 NLT).*

Elsie (Continued): Dr Carey, don't mind me. My priorities for now are still a work-in-progress. I will get there in the end like you, hopefully.

Elsie (to herself): As I went through the files, a million questions flashed through my mind as I saw Allison Blackwell's notes again. I didn't realise I was speaking to myself loudly.

Dr Carey: "Elsie, are you ok?"

Elsie: "Yes, I am fine. It's just that my mind is flooded with a million thoughts at the moment."

Elsie (Thinking and praying): O Lord, what should I do? I want to help this candidate, my friend, Allison. Is this coincidence or divine providence that she has applied to the same agency that I am requesting services from?

Should I take her into Mama Tamer's home? She seemed to be desperate for a live-in accommodation. However, is she mentally and emotionally stable to administer care to someone else? She seemed to be in need of care herself. Will she put my mother-in-law at risk? Will hiring her hinder or profit our relationship? Lord, I need your help.

Elsie (continued): As I sat there contemplating, scriptures began to flood my mind:

> *"Commit everything you do to the Lord. Trust him, and he will help you." (Psalm 37:5 NLT).*

> *"Commit your actions to the LORD, and your plans will succeed." (Proverbs 16:3 NLT)*

Elsie: Dr Carey, Guess what? I am feeling strongly about accepting one of the candidates that I happened to know years ago.

Dr Carey: How interesting! Have you ever thought that this might be divine providence rather than sheer coincidence? That it could be a result of answers to prayers. Maybe this shows it was meant to be.

Elsie: I hope so too Dr Carey. It would be great if it's divinely inspired.

Elsie (to herself quietly as she listened to Dr Carey): Lord, is this a confirmation?

> *"…The facts of every case must be established by the testimony of two or three witnesses. (2 Corinthians 13:1(b) NLT).*

Elsie (to herself): I didn't tell Dr Carey that I was in touch with Allison and maybe I should. He seemed to be a very wise and insightful person.

Dr Carey (Excited): "Who is it?" "Who is it?" "Please tell me a bit more!"

Elsie: Dr Carey, it's Allison Blackwell-Palmer. Years ago, we used to share the same dormitory at university. However, I would like just a bit more time. I would like to use my head to make the decision and not my heart alone. I want to confirm it with my husband, Les, so that we can both pray about it to see whether we have peace in making the final decision.

Dr Carey: If you need any further assistance in arriving at a decision, do let me know. I'm looking forward to hearing from you soon.

Elsie: Thanks Dr Carey. I will. It was a pleasure being at your office again today. It genuinely felt like I was in a lecture at a seminary.

Dr Carey (Smiled, shook my hand then said): "Best of luck, Elsie"

> *"Beg you a dollar Sir."*

> *"Beg you a dollar Ma'am."*

Those words kept echoing in my head as I left the office and reflected on Allison and our first meeting in the cafe as she walked along the rows of tables begging. My eyes began welling up again with tears of compassion, guilt and empathy. Maybe it was divine that I held on to the dollar and not gave it to her then. Maybe this is the real opportunity now for me to give her something more tangible and valuable. As you may well know, you can give and not love, but you cannot love and don't give. I love Allison; therefore, I need to employ her.

I jumped into my car but couldn't drive off for about 10 minutes. I wept and wept. Then, I was sure I heard a voice saying, "Elsie, are you ok?" I quickly dried my tears, smiled and looked up. But there was no one in sight. Goose pimples immediately covered my arms, and my head felt like it was doubled in size. I barely managed to gain composure then sped off home as if I was driving on one of Formula's 1 race track.

> *You can give and not love,*
> *but you cannot love and not give.*

And the story continues – see book 2

ACKNOWLEDGEMENTS

I would like to express my sincere gratitude to Daniella, Alliza Joy and Ana for the enthusiasm they showed in wanting to get the first opportunity to read and feedback their thoughts about this book. Your feedback proved invaluable.

I would also like to thank members of my church community, friends and colleagues, both present and former, who kept asking me for an update on the progress of my book. This has not only helped me to keep the vision alive, but it also kept me focused and inspired in wanting to fulfil it, amidst the demands of a busy work schedule and life itself.

Most of all, I would like to thank the Holy Spirit for the flow of inspiration, insight and perseverance in writing this book. It was bred out of a desire to touch the lives of others who are facing challenging and seemingly impossible situations by providing encouragement and hope.

It is also the hope that those who come into contact with the content of this book would both realise and recognise that there is a Source to turn to; and not to give up regardless of how despairing and debilitating their situations might seem.

Marner Housen

BIBLIOGRAPHY

Bible quotations:

All scriptures are taken from
https://www.biblegateway.com/passage/?search unless
otherwise indicated.
- The Holy Bible, New King James Version (NKJV),
  Copyright 2013, Holman Bible Publishers
- The Holy Bible, New Living Translation (NLT),
  Copyright 2008, Tyndale House Publishers, Inc.
- https://www.biblegateway.com/versions/New-
  International-Version-NIV-Bible/
- https://www.biblegateway.com/versions/New-Living
  -Version-NLV-Bible/
- https://www.biblegateway.com/versionsMessage-
  Version-MSG-Bible/
- https://www.biblegateway.com/versions/King-
  James-Version-KJV-Bible/
- (https://www.biblegateway.com/versions/Contempor
  ary-English-Version-CEV-Bible/
- https://www.biblegateway.com/versions/Modern -
  English -Version-MEV-Bible/

Dixon, Jesse "I am Redeemed." Accessed June, 20 2022
https://www.lyrics.com/lyric/14358857/Jessy+Dixon/I+Am
+Redeemed

Moore, Captain Tom. Favourite quotes: *"Tomorrow will be
a good day;*

"My today was all right and my tomorrow will certainly be better. That's the way I've always looked at life; "We will get through it."

<u>https://www.thesun.co.uk/news/13950581/captain-tom-moore-inspirational-quotes-words/</u> Accessed August 1, 2022.